Crime, Cash, Credit and Chaos

Colin McCall spent over four decades in the fields of education and training. In the course of his career he served in a variety of senior professional roles and published articles and books on a number of educational topics. Previous titles in this series include *Routes, Roads, Regiments and Rebellions: A brief history of the life and work of General George Wade (1673-1748) the Father of the Military Roads in Scotland.*

Crime, Cash, Credit and Chaos

A brief history of the life and work of John
Law (1671–1729) the Father of Credit Systems

written by

Colin McCall
illustrated by

Martin Wellard

Lesser Known Heroes

SOLCOL

Copyright © Colin McCall 2007
Illustrations © Martin Willard 2007
First published in 2007 by SOLCOL
6 Moorcroft, Chesterfield Rd, Matlock
Derbyshire DE4 5LL
www.amolibros.com/solcol

Distributed by Gardners Books, 1 Whittle Drive, Eastbourne, East
Sussex, BN23 6QH
Tel: +44(0)1323 521555 | Fax: +44(0)1323 521666

British Library Cataloguing in Publication Data
A catalogue record for this book is available from the British Library

ISBN 978-0-9544455-1-5

Typeset by Amolibros, Milverton, Somerset
This book production has been managed by Amolibros
Printed and bound by Advance Book Printing, Oxford, England

Contents

List of illustrations

Cover

John Law and key images relating to his life – the duel, his links with France and Louisiana, his banknote and one of his favourite places, the Rialto Bridge in Venice.

In the text

Acknowledgements

IT IS again a pleasure to thank my family for their continued interest in *Lesser Known Heroes* and the support that Margaret, Charlotte and Richard have given me when my spirit for the task has dipped. Martin Wellard has once more contributed quality illustrations that gracefully enhance the text and support the presentation.

I remain significantly indebted to staff who work in our wonderful public libraries – most particularly the members of staff at The British Library and those in the general and reference sections of the libraries at Birmingham, Chesterfield and Derby. It saddens me that such skilful and dedicated service may be lost as our libraries move ever closer to becoming shops rather than gateways for the public to good literary experience.

This book is for George and Violet McCall and Betsy and Ronald Turton. Though no longer with us, they are remembered with affection every day.

Preface

THE SERIES *Lesser Known Heroes* seeks to examine some of the ideas and actions contributed to our heritage by men and women who broadly speaking are less well known to the general public. The intention is to provide readable brief synopses on the characters behind the history. Every effort has been made to acknowledge the known evidence and to source as fully as possible key reference material.

The second book maintains the approach of moving outside the central text from time to time to set the chief character within the context of contemporary personalities and events. These sections entitled *historical connections* did appeal to many readers of the first book and it is hoped the strategy will find equal favour this time round.

As in the first text, this one also includes old English where this is deemed easily decipherable by the reader. This is done to preserve the voice of the time and to give it full historical validity.

Some of those commenting on the first book asked for more details about locations and sites worth visiting in relation to the history outlined. For this reason, and in recognition that a growing number of people now pursue 'active history' by using short breaks for intellectual stimulation, this book contains a 'John Law Trail'. This describes the significance of key locations in Edinburgh, Paris, London and Venice.

The information available on John Law is a mixture of known facts, conjecture and somewhat questionable, but possibly correct, tittle-tattle. I have sought to represent an accurate portrayal of the man and his achievements, but any errors remain my responsibility. The reader wishing to verify the picture presented here will find larger works on John Law in the bibliography.

Introduction

IF YOU had possessed sufficient money, time and literacy on Monday, 7th January 1695 to be reading the *London Gazette* – the following advertisement may well have caught your eye.

> 'Captain John Law, lately a prisoner in the King's Bench for murther, aged 26, a very tall black lean man, well shaped, above six feet high, large pock-holes in his face, big high nosed, speaks broad and loud, made his escape from the said prison. Whoever secures him so he may be delivered at the said prison, shall have fifty pounds paid immediately by the Marshall of the King's Bench.'

If you had survived the next twenty-six years and been in attendance at the King's Bench on the 28th November 1721, you would have heard the same John

Law plead his majesty's pardon for the murder of Edward Wilson. Whilst listening to the plea, it would not have escaped your attention that he was assisted on this occasion by influential people of the day, including some with titles, such as the Duke of Argyll and the Earl of Ilay.

Assuming you were acquainted with John in the two decades between these two events, you would have heard him express many other sentiments and you would know the many other descriptions attached to his name and character.

Taking sufficient literary licence to assume you were writing an obituary notice for him shortly after his death, you might choose to include such descriptors as *'a man of the rarest and most remarkable genius but one without virtue or religion'*[1], *'the eldest son of Satan'*[2], *'a gambler, a manipulator, a man of financial genius'*[3], *that reckless and unbalanced, but fascinating genius'*[4], *'the pleasant character mixture of swindler and prophet'*[5], *neither a quack nor a swindler, but a sophisticated promoter and a dauntless schemer'*[6], *'perhaps the most innovative financial scoundrel of all time'*.[7] Or, resisting the temptation to use the words of others you might have chosen to include some testimony from John's own self-assessment. Thus, in his final interview with the Duke of Orléans he is reported as saying: *'My lord, I acknowledge that I have committed great faults; I did so because I am a man, and all men are liable to err; but I declare to your royal highness that none of them proceeded from knavery and that nothing of that kind will be found in the whole course of my conduct.'*[8]

Allowing that one of your descendants some decades thereafter had obtained a place at university to read economics, he/she might have encountered other descriptions of John Law. They might come to agree with the statement that *'he worked out the economics of his projects with a brilliance and, yes, a profundity, which places him in the front rank of monetary theorists of all times'*,[9] or perhaps they would choose to affirm the statement that *'he was not a swindler, but an honest and misguided optimist'*.[10] If they had the opportunity to read widely on the subject of John Law and his monetary systems, they might conclude that he *'pre-empted much of modern monetary economics'*.[11] If, in parallel with economics they were reading psychology or sociology, they might also suggest that, despite a case for his economic prowess, it could also be concluded, with the benefits of modern hindsight, that at times he appeared to be a cunning opportunist and a misogynist.

At this temporal stage, your hypothetical family would know that both during his lifetime and in the time that has passed since, John Law attracted a diverse range of opinions about his character, his motives in life, his economic and business acumen, and indeed his courage and tenacity in the face of significant challenges and adversities.

Usually, such wide-ranging opinion about an individual suggests substantial capability, or great notoriety, or both. That is, the individual is remarkable, a rascal, or they present something of the two dispositions.

Let us proceed to unravel more facts about John Law to see if we can substantiate his inclusion in the gallery of 'lesser known heroes' – or if we are persuaded to reject him from residence there at the end of our sojourn.

Historical connection 1

The King's Bench sat in Westminster Hall from the time of Henry III until its absorption into the High Court in 1875. Though the name implies 'trial before the King', a monarch was seldom present. It was, however, the highest court of common law in England and Wales and throughout its many years of business it attracted cases ranging from treason to fairly trivial highway offences.

The 'Plea Side' dealt with civil issues, the 'Crown Side' with criminal. There was also an Exchequer. Despite the seriousness of its remit, it was not an elaborate or pretentious environment. ... *'each court consisted of a simple bench raised within a canopy and side curtain, a bench beneath for the officers of the court, a bar within which were assembled the Counsel, and outside stood the barristers and the public, The Chancery and King's Bench were stationed in the extreme end of the hall, opposite the great door, near which, in the north-west corner was the Common Pleas.*

The rest of the hall was taken up by the stalls of booksellers, fruiterers, and others, who plied their trade with as much zeal and noise as did the advocates higher up the hall.'[12]

The location of the court took on increased significance when the House of Commons acquired St Stephen's Chapel as their meeting place. This had to be approached through Westminster Hall, hence the Speaker *'always passed through Westminster Hall on his way to the House of Commons, and saluted the Courts of Common Pleas and King's Bench, the judges rising from their seats, with their caps on, to receive and return the Speaker's salute.'*[13]

John Law was in distinguished company in being tried in this setting. Famous judges of the King's Bench have included John More, Sir Edward Coke (1552-1643) and Sir John Holt (1642-1710). John More was the father of the executed and canonised Sir Thomas More (1478-1535). Coke tried Sir Walter Raleigh for treason – albeit at Chichester because of the Plague. He also prosecuted the members of the Gunpowder Plot. Holt was regarded in his time – and subsequently – as an unbiased and upright judge. He did much to bring to an end the trial of women for witchcraft.

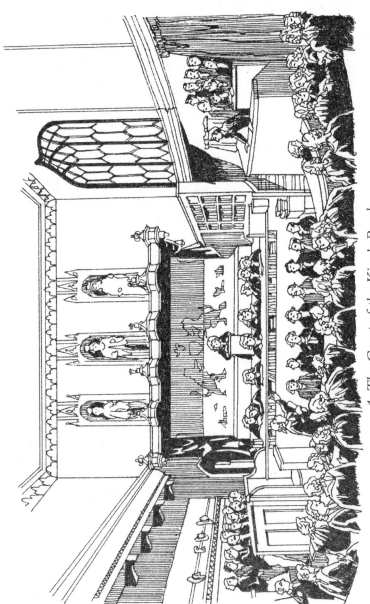

1 *The Court of the King's Bench.*

Conception to Crime

THE MARRIAGE between Jean Campbell and William Law brought John into the world. He was born in Edinburgh in the month of April 1671. For a person who in the course of his lifetime attracted fame and notoriety in abundance, his record of baptism is starkly plain.

21st of April 1671

William Law goldsmith, and Jean Campbell, a son named John. Witnesses: Mr John Law, John Law, goldsmith, Archibald Hislop, bookbinder, Heogh Campbell, John Melvill and John Murray, merchants.[1]

His father was dead before John reached his majority. His mother was to extract her son from a state of financial embarrassment just before he reached that milestone.

He was born into significant material comfort. His mother, William's second wife, brought a handsome dowry to the marriage and his father acquired wealth from his profession. They eventually had sufficient assets to purchase the estates of Lauriston and Randleston in the parish of Cramond near Edinburgh. The former included Lauriston Castle.

Historical connection 2

The original Lauriston Castle was built by Sir Archibald Napier of Merchiston. One of the Napiers was John the inventor of logarithms. The original building was a late sixteenth-century tower house but it has since gone through several alterations. Robert Dalgliesh the solicitor serving King Charles II bought the castle in 1656 and it was sold to William Law in 1683.

William Law had no time to enjoy Lauriston. He died in Paris after an unsuccessful operation to remove a stone, just as 1683 was drawing to a close. He is buried in the city in the chapel at Scots College.

John became laird of Lauriston and the bulk of the estate was left in trust until he reached his majority. He had left for London well before that day arrived.

The Laws, through their descendants, kept Lauriston until 1827. The last owners were the Reid family. They bequeathed the building and its contents to the people of Edinburgh. It is now a museum.

2   Lauriston Castle – before later modifications.

John was a day pupil at the Edinburgh High School until he was thirteen. He then went to Eaglesham, a boarding school in Renfrewshire. The son of the headmaster was married to John's sister, but the choice of Eaglesham was not founded essentially on the family connection. From an early age John was interested in physical sports, including the exercise to be enjoyed with the female form. The move to Eaglesham was in part related to the need to remove the locally named 'Jessamy John' from the temptations of the city. It was a suspension rather than a cure. While still legally a minor, but already expert in *all manner of debaucheries*[2] he went south in 1691 to London.

He soon chose to live in London, rather than return to Edinburgh. In the south he had near free reign to exercise his preferences for female company and gambling, occasionally offsetting these pleasures to undertake focused study on the principles and practice of finance.

At the time he arrived in London, coffee houses were increasing rapidly. Edward Lloyd had transferred his coffee interests to Lombard Street in 1691 and Thomas Slaughter opened his famous Slaughter's in St Martin's Lane in 1692. They were different emporiums to those we know today. Some served as centres for business transactions, or they provided support to businesses, an example being Edward Lloyd's clearance house for shipping information, which led to the internationally known Lloyd's of London. Other coffee houses developed reputations based on other business pursuits, Slaughter's becoming well-established around games associated with gambling, such as cards and chess. It is possible that Law may have met two notable characters of the day. John Campbell, a goldsmith, who in 1692 set up the business at the Three Crowns in the Strand that later became Coutts' Bank, and Abraham de Moivre, a mathematician, who supplemented his academic income by attending coffee houses to advise card players on the known rules of probability.

John took comfortable lodgings in St Giles-in-the-Fields, an area incorporating the current districts of Bloomsbury, Convent Garden and Holborn. At the time he went there the area had as many contrasts as it does today. It housed those with affluence and rank, those who set fashion trends, and those in less favoured circumstances, such as poor refugees from Ireland and France who made what living they could in the dingy alleyways and less salubrious abodes.

The area had many gaming houses and John frequented these. He found more than enjoyment in these fashionable settings. He applied his critical acumen to the most popular games, including working out the odds for and against different combinations of the dice. Alas, neither his instincts nor his scientific approach provided a viable gambling career at this stage in his life, although he was to become very successful in this enterprise later. Shortly before he came of age, he agreed a debt rescue package with his mother. Part of the agreement included selling to his mother his interest in the Lauriston and Randleston estates.

Mr Law made a conveyance of the eftate of Lauriston to his mother, in confequence of certain fums advanced to him; that conveyance is dated 6th February, 1692, he being then, as the difpofition bears, in London.[3]

The money from the sale of his Edinburgh assets sustained his lavish London lifestyle. His prowess as a rake continued unabated, even if his progress as a gambler was not as successful. One of his longer-term affairs was with a Mrs Lawrence who was regularly present at Law's lodgings to the point where another lady resident objected to the arrangement. This lady was said to be the sister of a well-known London 'beau' Edward Wilson. Wilson, though from a very modest background, spent lavishly and enjoyed a luxurious lifestyle.

> Beau Wilson, a person who, by the common report of fame, kept a coach and six horses – maintained his family in great splendour and grandeur, being full of money – no one complaining of his being their debtor, yet from whence he had the effects which caused him to appear in so great an equipage, is hard to determine.[4]

The source of Wilson's wealth has been the subject of much conjecture. Some accounts suggest it derived from his being the 'hired lover' of Elizabeth Villiers, the favourite of the monarch William III. Others suggest that Wilson may have been in a homosexual relationship with a rich admirer.

Whatever the source of Wilson's riches and his connection with John Law, the two men fought a duel in a relatively deserted part of the neighbourhood. Some say that Elizabeth Villiers encouraged a 'bloody settlement' out of fear that Wilson was threatening to expose their largesse. Others point to an ongoing feud of some kind between the two men. There is also the possibility the fight was over money or to avenge a slur of some kind that had passed between them.

How well the two men were matched is not known, but Law had been skilful with the rapier from an early age. According to the eyewitnesses, he despatched Wilson almost immediately, making a two-inch deep fatal wound to the stomach.

Historical connection 3

Men have used sticks, stones, spears and swords to defend themselves, to settle disagreements and to square debts of honour since time immemorial. Trial by combat was used to prove just cause in the sight of God well into medieval times, the simple logic being that divine acceptance of the 'right cause' dictated the winning adversary. In 1386 a trial by combat placed *a knight against a squire accused of violating the knight's beautiful young wife*. Defeat of her husband dictated her fate also, since if he *lost the duel, she would be put to death as a false accuser*.[5]

The distinctiveness of a duel as an act of aggression lay in the pre-arranged rules that were followed and the fact that the combat was often seen as an alternative to any form of legal justice. Indeed, in the Middle Ages, the two processes could be united, since a judge could order a duel and demand that the adversaries place sureties to guarantee their appearance at the appointed place and time.

In most European countries, duelling became a common and accepted way of 'seeking satisfaction' when the rapier evolved from the cut-and-thrust sword. Pistols replaced swords, as the technology of personal armament rolled on, and the development of firearms effectively brought an end to life-terminating fights with just cold steel.

If called to a duel, it was not easy to refuse. In general, women, the infirm and men below twenty or over sixty were exempt, but the majority of other men had to answer, or find someone who was willing to take their place.

The practice of duelling did not go uncontested. Most European countries had legislation in place forbidding duels by the 1600s, the French from the twelfth century, but the law was rarely enacted. Though King Louis XIII did execute a group of duellists for settling a challenge on the Place Royale in 1627, this was because the dispute was viewed essentially as disrespect to the king's honour rather than merely disregard of the law.

Serious frowning upon duelling seems to have occurred earlier in England than in Ireland and the rest of Europe. The practice moved towards extinction in England from around 1819 to 1836. By this time, the law had definitely placed the outcomes of the contest in the categories of assault, manslaughter or murder. The jail terms were extensive or the victor might be pursued in the civil courts for extensive damages.

A fascinating account of some famous duels and their humorous or unfortunate consequences can be found in Holmes.[6] Hutton also traces the history of the practice with the sword, its demise through the development of pistol duelling and its continuation in sporting guise through the art of fencing. [7]

Law pleaded not guilty to the murder of Wilson. He described the incident as one of self-defence, Wilson having drawn his sword first. However, in summing up, the judge, Sir Salathiel Lovell, directed the jury to the 'continual quarrel carried on betwixt them' and although this does not appear to have been true, Law was found guilty of murder. He was sentenced on 22nd April 1694 to death by hanging.

He had powerful influences working to stay his execution. First, as in most other European countries, there was an ambivalent attitude to duelling and the Royal prerogative of clemency was often exercised. Second, in this case Elizabeth Villiers may have used her charms to persuade her royal lover to influence where he could in order to prevent any unfortunate confession before or on the way to the scaffold. Third, John Law asked noblemen of Scotland to intercede on his behalf.

The result was a reprieve but not liberty. Edward Wilson's brother lodged an appeal in the Court of the King's Bench and still cited murder. Law appeared at Westminster Hall on 22nd June to answer to the renewed indictment. The eminence of his counsel is a measure of the material and other influence he could draw on at this time. The senior group included Sir William Thompson who had been involved in the trial of Lord Mohan. He had also killed someone in a duel, the victim being the actor William Mountford.

Law's representative argued legal technicalities and the court reserved time to consider these and other rulings. This took the case across the long vacation and Law was returned to the King's Bench Prison to wait the autumn legal term.

Historical connection 4

The King's Bench Prison was located in Borough High Street, Southwark. It was a private institution not directly under government control. Prisoners paid for the officers and their keep. Those indicted on civil offences could pay a large sum and serve their sentences outside the prison, so long as they remained within three miles of it. There was also a 'release fee' and it is said that if this was not found, the sentence continued indefinitely. This scurrilous profit-making continued until the Home Office took over the prison in 1877.

> The walls of the prison are very high and all prospect beyond them is excluded, even to the uppermost windows... . The rooms are nearly all alike and measure about 9 feet square. The building, which is constructed of brick, is very extensive; and the marshal, who has the keeping of this prison, has very handsome apartments on the outside. ... such as are able to purchase the liberties may have the benefit of

> walking through the borough and in St George's fields.[8]
>
> The Borough High Street gaol was demolished in 1754 but a larger replacement was attached to the Court of Kings Bench. It was also used to confine mostly those convicted of debt and libel.

Because duels were regarded by the courts as premeditated acts, and hence murder, Law's crime did not permit him to purchase any liberty. He was confined within the prison itself, where security seems to have waned between a fairly lax regime and rather more draconian measures. Thus, in the first three months awaiting the continuation of his new trial, Law had filed down several bars of his cell window – but upon these being discovered, he was placed in irons and these were retained on him when he next appeared at the Court of King's Bench.

The outcome was a disappointment for the duellist offender. His counsel lost on technicalities and his case was put off until the New Year of 1695. Law's friend's came to his aid, and they seem to have been able and willing to get him various instruments and possibly potions to help his escape. The level and range of this assistance, coupled with the fact that the description issued after his escape was grossly inaccurate, suggests help again from the king's mistress or other influential persons, including possibly a 'blind eye' from King William himself.

If the door was not opened for him, Law faced a thirty-foot drop to reach the outside. By whatever means, he made it. With the help of a coach to carry him away speedily, the lithe, handsome, softly spoken and bold-spirited Scot, now somewhat dishevelled, made his escape to the Continent. No doubt some people looked around to turn in for the reward, 'a very tall black man with pock holes in his face and who spoke broad and low'. They looked in vain.

Historical connection 5

Elizabeth Villiers was one of six daughters born to Lady Frances and Colonel Edward Villiers. The family lived at Richmond in a property granted by Charles II. They were joined at Richmond by the six-year-old Princess Anne after the death of her mother. Despite her apparent distance in line for the throne, Anne was destined to become Queen. However, that possibility seemed remote at the time she joined Lady Frances, her nominated governess, at the Villiers' home.

By the marker of physical beauty, Elizabeth Villiers was not well endowed. She had a significant squint and other physical imperfections. Friends and enemies often described her as plain, wrinkly

---

and prone to girth. However, she had the longer-lasting qualities of character and resolve. She became a good friend of Jonathan Swift, the author of *Gulliver's Travels* and he attributed to her the saying that '*in men, desire begets love, and in women, love begets desire*' – more crudely interpreted nowadays as 'men want sex, women want love'. Swift also described her as the '*wisest woman I ever saw*'.[9]

Elizabeth became a mistress for William III while she was serving as one of the ladies-in-waiting to his wife. Her husband received the title Earl of Orkney; hence others who knew Elizabeth later refer to her as Lady Orkney or the Countess of Orkney.

It is said that she used to wear a mask and insist on the light of one candle for her alleged assignations with Beau Wilson. This was mainly to protect her identity. However, she must have been conscious of the negative reactions to her physical features (no portrait of her ever emerged), and the cloak-and-dagger element may also have appealed to her distinct spirit of adventure.

John Law always denied she had been directly involved in his prison escape, but others point to the nature of the escape and to the false advert as evidence of the influence of a powerful friend. The advert was clearly designed to mislead and to enhance rather than hinder Law's chances of escape.

Elizabeth Villiers did have the attention and the ears of many powerful men of the time. The fact that John Law never did describe the plan for and nature of his escape suggests he had entered into a bond of silence on the matter, or he was determined to protect well-known people. The other explanations for how Beau Wilson came into his money and the fatal link he had with John Law are all tenable,[10/11] but in the absence of specific truth, there is no reason not to accept the possibility that Elizabeth Villiers had some significant influence.

Elizabeth founded a school in Cork in 1709 and advised various members of the early Hanoverian Court. One of her last ceremonial appearances was at the coronation of King George II in 1727. Those rather unkind to her appearance recorded further comments on the nature of her very large and now aged figure. Perhaps they were blind to the 'inner lady' who Macaulay said *had many fine qualities*.[12] Lady Orkney died in Albermarle Street on 19th April 1733.

Travels to Triumph

THERE IS some uncertainty surrounding John Law's whereabouts in the first decade following his escape from King's Bench Prison. It is known that he made his way to the Continent and roamed around there. He spent his time gambling and studying financial systems.

'It is extremely difficult to trace his movements since none of his correspondence for these years has survived, the evidence of his contemporaries is scanty and there are few references in his own later writings to his activities at this time. According to his first and contemporary anonymous biographer, he made his way to France immediately after his escape from the King's Bench Prison. But France and England were then at war, and in view of that fact it is difficult to believe that he was able to put in at any French port at this time. The

Jacobite agents, who regularly passed between the ex-king James II's Court at St. Germains and the exiled monarch's supporters in Britain, travelled as a rule through the Low Countries and it is practically certain that Law, in eventually making his way to Paris as he did, used this route. Furthermore, French authorities seem agreed that he did not visit France until after peace had been signed between the two countries over two years later. It is more likely that Law used this interval to acquire the detailed knowledge of Dutch banking of which he was later to give proofs in his writings.[1]

Though Law had acquired knowledge of the newly founded Bank of England, both before and during his time in London, the Bank of Amsterdam was around a century older. The efforts made by King William III as William Prince of Orange to adhere a league of nations in opposition to French expansionary ideals also made The Hague the centre of important diplomatic exchanges. This meant the Dutch location was ideal for Law's financial studies, but as an alleged (though not actual) Jacobite sympathiser he may have kept a low profile and operated largely incognito. Though it is stated that Law worked *'for some time as secretary to the British resident in Holland'*[2] it is difficult to find evidence to substantiate this claim.

Venice had established a bank in 1587 and a Rotterdam financier named Wissel had tried to import the principles and structure of Italian banking to Holland in 1598.[3] This first attempt was unsuccessful but it did lay a path for the foundation of the Bank of Amsterdam in 1609. By the time Law arrived, the city had a strong and celebrated banking establishment. The system was essentially paper notes for coins. The exchange was based on the weight of the coin not their existing currency value. The notes formed a strong basis of trust between customers and the bank on one hand, and traders on the other. The fact that they were redeemable against the true original value of the coins exchanged for them meant they tended to incur a slight profit for the owner on the open market. Law described his view of the arrangement:

'The Dutch…set up the bank of Amsterdam. Their Money was Silver, but their trade was so great as to find payments even in Silver inconvenient. This Bank like that of Sweedland, is a secure place, where Merchants may give in Money, and have credit to trade with. Besides the convenience of easier and quicker Payments, these Banks saves the Expense of Casheers, the Expense of Bags and Carriage, losses by bad money, and the money is safer than in the Merchants Houses, for 'tis less liable to Fire or Robbery, the necessary Measures being taken to prevent them.

People who have Money in the Bank of Amsterdam, and People of other Countries who deal with them, are not liable to Changes in the Money, by its being allay'd or alter'd in the Denomination: for the Bank receives no Money but what's of Value, and is therefore call'd Bank-money; and tho rais'd in current payments, it goes for the value pledg'd for in Bank-payments. The Agio of the Bank changes a Quarter or half per cent as current Money is more or less scarce.'[4]

Historical connection 6

Paper money and coin are not direct tangible wealth. The wealth lies in what they can be exchanged for. They may be exchanged for goods, labour, a contract of service that is to be delivered, or one already received. In general, all forms of money are a 'promise' and the currency value of the money lasts only as long as the trust lasts.

Coins became a way of representing the trust from very early times. They could be easily stored or carried around and as harder metals came into being these were used in the production of coins because of their durability. Wealth or trade exchange was represented in some form of metal

---

from around 2000BC and forerunners of more modern coins were used as far back as 690BC.

The use of precious metals bestowed further significance to coinage. The use of valuable material had the advantage of projecting status and implying true value, but the introduction of precious metals also increased abuse. Common misdemeanours included counterfeiting (using precious metal only to plate the coin leaving the inner debased) and providing underweight coins by carefully clipping the edges. Since many coins had royal recognition or were instrumental in guaranteeing the trust underpinning trade, convicted forgers normally received capital punishment. The execution might be by tortuous means such as being *boiled in oil*.[5]

Paper money can be traced to China in around the seventh century AD and it was in significant use in Sichuan by the eleventh century. As with coinage, those producing or circulating counterfeit money faced severe penalties. The punishment for attempting to forge John Law's banknotes (1716) was death.[6]

The use of paper money increased when it became inconvenient or too risky to carry large amounts of heavy coin around, and when the paper notes became more difficult to copy.

Preventing forgery of paper notes has been a scientific and technological enterprise since the 1790s. In 1809, Joseph Bramah designed a press for the Bank of England and this allowed the date and a unique number to be placed on plate-printed notes. Various water marks were tried in the early 1800s but the Bank of England's chief engraver copied them easily. It was not until Jacob Perkins in the USA developed hardened engraved steel that a more secure master die gave better protection. The use of colour printing, more complex machine engraving, pictorial representation and the insertion into notes of a metal thread followed. Ultra-violet light and foil holograms are more modern techniques to add security to the exchange of notes.[7]

Other systems of trust were also developing in parallel with money. The use of 'letters of credit' between people who trusted each other was commonplace by medieval times, and the 'bill of exchange' was developed in north Italy to provide an accredited transfer of funds without the necessity to ship coin. The first cheque issued in England appeared in London in 1659.

Money replaced the clumsiness of direct barter, whereby cattle, crops, salt and manufactured curios were exchanged directly for other commodities. In general, the use of banking and coins was spread by economic activity, trade agreements and military conquests. The link between warfare and finance has always been strong and the word *pay* comes from the Latin word meaning to *pacify*.[8] Equally, until more formal conscription, no leader or monarch could guarantee an army of standing without obvious hard currency to pay wages.

Let's not be subject to vain delusion
Of those who would have us fight without pay
While money chinks My Captain Ile obey.[9]

The word *bank* is thought to derive from the Italian word for bench – i.e. *banco* – since the dominant merchant and banking groups of the fourteenth and fifteenth centuries resided in the states of Florence and Lombardy and their business was conducted at counters or formal benches.[10]

During the eighteenth and nineteenth centuries private and national banks took over the middle ground of 'promise' – this being enshrined in their stated pledge 'to pay the bearer on demand the sum of'. Law was describing the means whereby the Bank of Amsterdam offered to redeem 'credit' passed on in their name, somewhat like underwriters of cheques and credit cards do today. The security lies essentially in the trust of the system and the capacity of banks to redeem the credit, if called upon so to do.

Law was a fugitive from English law. This meant he could set foot in Scotland without too much fear of abduction, or the risk of being sent back to London to face the consequences of his escape. After ten years roaming the Continent, he was anxious to see his mother again, especially since it had been reported to him that she was in very poor health. He arrived back in Scotland probably early in 1704 to find that his mother had made a will bequeathing him the family estates. He was accompanied to Scotland by his current lover, one Katherine Knowles. She may have been the sister of Charles Knollys who had been an inmate of the King's Bench Prison at the same time as Law. Charles Knollys had also killed a man in a duel. This was the brother-in-law of Knolly's first wife. This gallant soul had tried, without success, to seek common-law justice for Knolly's desertion of Elizabeth Lister almost immediately after he had married her.

Whether Charles introduced Katherine to Law or the

two met co-incidentally is not known. It is clear that Katherine was married to another then and known as Katherine Seigneur. She arranged an elopement with Law and they set off together for Genoa in Italy. Given her aristocratic background, her existing material benefits and Law's notoriety, it would have been clear to her that there was no roundabout ahead. For Law this relationship seemed to move him beyond the role of opportunist philanderer.

3   *Katherine Law.*

The couple had two children, John and Mary Katherine, but when and where they were born is not clear. It is possible that young John was being carried by Katherine when she went with Law to Scotland. What is known is that by the mores of the day, the children were illegitimate, a circumstance that was to be disadvantageous to them after their father's death.

John and Katherine were soon living in style, thanks to his cunning speculation in foreign currency exchange and his skill at gambling. It was from these favourable material circumstances they made their way to Scotland.

John and Katherine appear to have settled down very well in Edinburgh and even the health of John's mother improved with their presence. John felt sufficiently content with his lot to petition Queen Anne for a pardon. He stated 'your petitioner is debarred from serving Your Majesty (as he is most desirous)' and he added that Beau Wilson's brother had agreed to drop the action of appeal. In fact, Law had worked very hard on influential friends to get Robert Wilson to this state of mind. Alas, it was to no avail. The petition came back in September endorsed 'Rejected'.

Although this was a downward turn of events, John did not have to flee. Scotland's government and legislature were then separate to those in England and as long as he stayed north of the border he could live and work as a free man.

Whether it was being home again in Edinburgh, the beginnings of family joys and family responsibilities, the troubled state of the Scottish economy, or a combination of these influences, Law now turned his mind to more serious intellectual pursuit. He published anonymously the essay *Money and Trade Considered with a Proposal for Supplying the Nation with Money*.

4   *John Law's paper* Money and Trade Considered
(1705).

The paper carries what appears at first glance to be a
pretentious imprimatur – *Printed by the Heirs and
Successors of Andrew Anderson, Printers to the Queens most
Excellent Majesty.* The obvious conclusion was that Law
was hedging his bets. First, he thought the author really
would be 'discovered' by those on high. Second, they
would applaud the clear and strong arguments in the
essay. Third, they would appreciate the style and form
of presentation, since it mirrored some of the official
publications of the day. The reality may be more
mundane. Andrew Anderson was a relative within the
Law dynasty. He was married to a sister of John's mother.

Although Anderson had died in 1676, in 1661 he had been granted a forty-one year seal by Charles II to work as the 'King's Printer'. Law may have felt secure in presenting his paper to a firm that still had foundations in and obligations to the extended family.

The paper was the second writing by Law on monetary matters. In 1704, he had produced a written proposal for the English parliament outlining the benefits of 'land money' over silver money. This paper was titled *Essay on a Land Bank* and like the later *Money and Trade* it is regarded as an accomplished and consistent economic argument.

He states a belief that land money is more secure than silver money. Land is safer as collateral and more flexible as a commodity. It also tends to be more stable, economically speaking, than the precious metals. These vary significantly in value with demand and supply, and can be more easily manipulated at the price level by those who control access and distribution. Equally, the value of precious metals is attributed in part to the quality they present with. Like any valuable artefact or treasure, they can deteriorate in quality and hence in value. He thought land to be more stable in this respect, and hence more suitable as the basis of the money.

> All goods being liable to changes in their value these goods whose value is most certain, or, least liable to changes are as to the value most qualified to be made money.[11]

He thought that money linked to land would be more elastic than currencies tied to finite 'reserves' such as gold and silver. In November 1789, the French revolutionary government pursued a similar line of thinking. They used the lands seized from the Church as security for bonds. These bonds were called *assignats* because purchasers were ostensibly 'assigned' a portion of land when they redeemed their bonds. Such ownership was pretence rather than a deliverable reality.

For Law, the 'reserves' of land would be all the land a country had that could be utilised for different functions. In an overall sense, land was likely to be far more substantial than 'precious' reserves. The former arrangement made monetary expansion easier.

> The credit of the land mint may be extended equal to the value of the whole lands in the nation.[12]

From his two papers, Law shaped a proposal to establish a trading corporation and to develop the use of paper money. This proposal went before the Parliament in Edinburgh but the proposed scheme was rejected. Before John could attract further support for revisions to his initial ideas, political circumstances overtook him. It became clear that a union was to take place between Scotland and England. The commencement of this would place Law back in the category of escaped prisoner with a debt of incarceration to pay. He fled back to the Continent.

James VI of Scotland became James I of England in 1603. His succession reduced 'two crowns' to one and this event is regarded as the first step of real union between Scotland and England. In terms of day-to-day reality, the union was nominal rather than substantial, and before and during the Civil War there were tensions and divisions. As in England, loyalties were split between those Scots who fought for the Crown and those who surrendered Charles I to the English parliament in 1647. During the time of the Protectorate (1654-1660) the union was marginal and temporary at best, and in 1701 the Scottish parliament refused to accept the Hanoverian succession.

The perceived threat from this lack of acceptance was the possibility of Scotland supporting a return of the Stuart dynasty (as many Scots did in 1715 and 1745 without success). The English parliament tried to nip the threat in the bud by moving legislation to create a real and stronger union. This legislation was enacted in the union act of 1707.

Concessions had to be made to the people of 'North Britain' and the act allowed Scotland to retain its church and its legal system. The Scots were also allowed free trade with England. The crosses of St George and St Andrew were blended into a 'Union flag'. This became known euphemistically as the 'Union Jack', after it started appearing on the jackstaff on 'men-of war' vessels. The red saltire of Patrick was added to the flag in 1801.

John Law did not wait for the 1707 act to become statute. He decided that the demise of the Scottish Parliament would jeopardise his freedom. He left Scotland with Katherine some time during 1706. Financially speaking, the move was a successful one:

> ...he again betook himself to the continent where he became so successful in his gambling ventures, particularly in Rome, Venice and Genoa, that in 1717 he had amassed a fortune of £110,000 sterling.[13]

Law's departure from Scotland occurred at the time the French Government was recognising that its finances were in dire straits. The following is a very concise summary of fiscal circumstances in France at the time.

The finances of France...were...in a serious condition. The public debt was colossal, and revenue failed to balance expenditure. Orléans (Regent) was unwilling to go to the length of formal repudiation of the debt, but a tribunal was established to investigate the conduct of the financiers, many of whom were ordered to refund large sums of money. Some loans were cancelled, and the interest on others was reduced, but the state gained little from such measures, since their effect was to lower the public credit. Some attempt was made to reduce public expenditure, but that of the court was untouched, and no material improvement was effected in the financial position.[14]

Following the protracted wars, many of the populace had low morale and the country as a whole was lacking vision and vitality. Unemployment escalated rapidly and even the nation's troops went without pay, so they roamed about scavenging what they could. Those with money hid it or put it into safe-keeping. Debts were left unpaid and new ones acquired in unfavourable circumstances. Louis XIV's last statement to his five-year-old great-grandson was a tragic reminder of the challenge he was leaving the nation. *Try to remain at peace with your neighbours I have loved war too much.*[15] Overall, at the end of his reign, France had lost much of its natural wealth and the monarchy no longer had the love and trust of the subjects.

Commerce was prostrate, manufactures were stagnant, agriculture had almost been abandoned. To escape service in the army or starvation at home, many labourers had fled to Italy. Deserted farms were to be frequently met with, and there were vast stretches of uncultivated land where the traveller encountered neither peasants nor domestic animals. The credit of the monarchy was almost gone.[16]

Adding to this negative state of affairs was the reluctance of wealthier individuals and fiscal groups to engage in financing the state. This reluctance flowed from many tributaries. First, the existing currency mechanisms were often manipulated to allow the state to obtain and multiply credit. Second, there were significant oscillations in the nature of the actual money around and in its financial viability (for example, minted new coins were seldom enough in value or quantity to cover surrendered old coins or substitute goods), resulting in the issuing of money certificates that depreciated rapidly. Third, though the government would use such certificates to pay central bills or debt, it would not accept them as payment for tax liabilities. Fourth, those with more fiscal acumen were worried that France might borrow ever-greater sums to finance more war and internal regal magnificence. Fifth, the value of coinage and the *billets de monnaie* were fluctuating in a manner that led to increasing bankruptcies and to anxiety or panic in investors. Sixth, there were few figures in the government, or indeed the country, with significant financial expertise and the power to stabilise the currency and the commercial markets. Seventh, as in all such periods of instability, the climate bred unscrupulous profiteers who scooped up large rake-offs or who brazenly used the financial systems *to lend the government its own money!*[17]

Philippe, Duc d'Orléans had been appointed by Louis XIV as Regent until the five-year-old Louis XV was old enough to maintain the crown and to provide for

5   *Philippe, Duc d'Orléans.*

its continuation. Philippe was expected to share his power with a nominated council, but with the consent of the *parlement* of Paris he took the full powers to himself.

It now fell to him to stem the tide of fiscal destruction. He brought with him the reputation of a debauchee, philanderer and rake. There were also those who believed he had poisoned the King and other members of the royal household. He was seen by many as unsuitable to the task of government because of his continual engagement in seduction and the constant hangovers he suffered after frequent drunken revelries.

> Philippe was aged forty-one at the time of his uncle's death (Louis XIV), but he looked older. Debauchery and too many drunken evenings had taken their toll. His left arm had been smashed by a cannonball in the wars, and his eyesight had deteriorated to the point where he had to peer so closely at documents that his quill pen became entangled in his wig. He was less careful about his dress then he had been, provoking Saint-Simon to quip that no one had less work to do than his Royal Highness's master of the wardrobe, except his confessor.[18]

Philippe was not without intellectual and diplomatic qualities. He handled the child king-in-waiting with pastoral sensitivity and skill, and he brought to an end the wars that had been ruining France. He was also a serious patron of the arts. He sponsored Voltaire's writing, he supported the royal library and he was instrumental in promoting French Rococo. He set the trend for aristocrats to live in Paris rather than Versailles. This aristocratic following sought rich living quarters with elegant Rococo interiors. There are some artefacts from this period in the Musée Carnavalet in Paris.

Orléans certainly appreciated the magnitude of the financial crisis facing the country and he threw himself into reversing the slide into fiscal calamity. At first, he fell back on time-honoured ways of dealing with fiscal problems. A new Financial Council was established. The administration of state finance was tightened and set within new audit measures. Steps were taken to reduce waste and increase the amount of tax revenue. The demobilisation of troops was speeded up and economies were introduced into both civil and military departments. Those holding state bonds had to place them with a commission for review. The bonds usually came back worth less than when they were sent in.

'This was in effect a partial state bankruptcy, and though it helped to reduce state obligations, it had a lamentable effect on public confidence, which fell to abysmal levels. Few wished to trust a government which utilized every trick in the book to escape or reduce its financial commitments... . The Chamber of Justice of

1716 performed ritualistic but largely symbolic damage on the hated figure of the corrupt state financier. The largest fines – 12 million livres overall – were levied on Antoine Crozat and Samuel Bernard, but both men lived to fight another day. In general, punishment rained down on the sprats, leaving most big fish able to swim away relatively undamaged. [19]

The fines were mainly imposed to placate the French public who believed that tax collectors took very large commissions from what they gathered in. In reality, though the state financiers and tax collectors were loathed by the public in general, their relationship with the government was complex. For example, those providing money were members of the nobility, their relations, or agents acting on behalf of this privileged group. It was necessary to keep their goodwill to secure loans to bolster up the fragile state finance.

> The financial system relied on the Court nobility and the provincial elites for funds…these were made available through the nobles own agents, who were the principal financiers.[20]

Overall the imposed mixture of more efficient accounting, more frugal financial management, and the punishment of some people alleged to have engaged in financial wrongdoing, did have a small effect. However, though a little public confidence was restored, major difficulties remained. There was no real boost to the war torn economy, the government remained largely dependent on suspect private financiers for the large part of its wealth, the financial straitjacket was further tightened by a period of restrictive spending, and war with Spain went potentially back and forth across the horizon.

Furthermore, in order to sustain social and political stability, the Regent had to live hand in glove with aristocratic interest. This meant that fair and proportionate taxation was never introduced as one of the strategies in the programme of economic reform. By and large, the sum of the steps taken amounted to little more than tinkering at the edges with an inequitable and increasingly unstable financial system.

By 1715, Orléans knew that he required a more radical approach. He also knew that important keys lay in restoring public confidence still further, whilst reconstituting state financial powers, so that they appeared less oscillatory and less threatening to the individual purse. Essentially, strong public confidence would lay a foundation for enlisting credit from broader ranks of people than the cartel of state financiers. Overall, something unique was required. A scheme to turn around the stagnating economy, lessen the financial crisis and liquidate the still escalating royal debt.

Philippe had met John Law in a gambling den, but

though gambling was well ingrained in Law the man, the Regent is unlikely to have taken him into his confidence on the basis of this association alone.

> This image of Law the gambler is one that none of his biographers have attempted to challenge. It is either accepted as a foible, perhaps even a major defect of his character, or alternatively used as a colourful adjunct of his personality. No one seems to have seen the paradox of how Law the gambler could metamorphose into Law the serious economist and policy-maker. No one seems to have asked why Philippe, duc d'Orléans…a serious and concerned politician, would have wanted to hand over the domain of economic policy making to such an apparently imbalanced individual whose actions seemed to be dominated by the goddess of chance.[21]

It is probable that Philippe saw and admired in Law his own foibles and the strong intellectual capacity they shared. He was clearly impressed with Law's seemingly clear thinking on financial policy and he was aware that other influential figures in his circle recommended Law as an ingenious and bold financier. Whatever the motives, the influence was strong because in a short space of time Philippe had entrusted John with the intricacies of the State debt. This included telling him that, in his capacity as Regent, he had been advised to cope with the debt by declaring total bankruptcy. Law was firmly against this proposal. He told Philippe:

> ...that an act of bankruptcy would cause greater confusion and would create more difficulty than there was in trying to arrange payment of the debt; that an unworthy bankruptcy would bring dishonour to the State; that the King and his successors would never again obtain any assistance from their subjects; that it would be a gross mistake to think that crushing his creditors would bring relief to his subjects, the means of relieving them being absent; that the loss would be felt by all of a Kingdom, there are also the invisible links which universally distribute the good and the bad; that all debts among individuals would beyond doubt be handled in the same way as the King's; that it was a matter of adding one group of ruined people to others; that means of subsistence would be lacking to all those whom the others kept in subsistence before the bankruptcy; that domestic and foreign commerce, arts and manufacturing would cease for want of purpose; that agriculture would be limited to the feeding only of out of work inhabitants; finally, the King would be poorer and less puissant, after having acquitted his debts through a bankruptcy, than he had been before.[22]

This comprehensive insight into the potential effects of State declared bankruptcy shows the power and depth of Law's financial understanding. On the strength of this and other advice, he was invited to the Court of France. It was not long before the Scot was entrusted with reorganising the country's finances.

At first things did not go smoothly. Law quickly put forward a proposal to establish a bank, but it was rejected. There was not sufficient confidence in the foundation he proposed. The lack of confidence is clear in the report of an extraordinary meeting held on 24th October 1715.

The idea of this bank is to cause all the revenues of the king to be brought to the bank; to give to the receivers and farmers of the taxes notes for ten crowns, one hundred crowns, and one thousand crowns, weight and standard of this day, which will be called bank-notes. These notes will be thereupon carried by the said receivers and farmers to the royal treasury, which will furnish them with receipts on account. All those to who payments are due from the king will receive at the royal treasury only bank notes, with which they can go at once to the bank to receive their value, no person being obliged to keep them or to receive them in trade. But the Sieur Lass [Law] pretends that their utility will be such that everybody will be glad to have them in preference to silver, on account of the ease with which payments in paper can be made, and on account of the assurance of receiving payment for them whenever it is desired.[23]

Given the very fluid state of royal finances at the time and in the immediate past, it is perhaps not surprising that a bank founded on royal funds and to be administered in the name and with the authority of the king should be regarded sceptically, especially when it was to be based on a new system of exchange. No one seemed inclined to support the idea of a bank where the promissory paper notes would only be guaranteed by the king. Opposition was strong and led by the Duke of Noailles. He was in an influential position, being principally in charge of French finances at the time. The Regent deferred, agreeing with the duke that it was necessary to win support for the idea of a bank before there would be sufficient credit forthcoming to sustain it.

Law then moved to offer himself for the lack of confidence. He submitted another proposal for a bank, this one to be based on his credit and those deposits he could secure from interested individuals. He saw this bank being independent of direct regal control but subject to inspection by agents representing the government. He hoped for a strong relationship between the king and the bank and worked to press the idea of bills from his bank forming legal tender between government and subjects. This proposal met with more success and Law signed a contract with the government in May 1716 allowing him to set up a 'Banque Générale' or General Bank. This became the 'Royal Bank' in 1718. The bank was an imitation of the Bank of England and despite the severe restrictions imposed on its organisation and *modus operandi,* after a faltering start it was successful. Branches of the bank opened in Amiens, Lyons, Orleans, Rochelle and Tours.

In essence, Law set up a state-chartered bank. This had the power to issue unbacked paper currency. This was done because Law believed that credit and the money supply was determined by the needs of trade and the economy in general. This position was in sharp contrast to those who assumed that the supply of money was controlled by the import of gold and by the state of trade balance. Law thought that an increase in the quantity of money would stimulate economic production, leading to a revival of both home industry and overseas trade. He was leading on an idea later succinctly described by Benjamin Franklin as '*money makes money, and the more money that money makes, makes more money'*;[24] though Franklin himself did not believe that paper currency alone could be substituted for silver or gold.

By 1718, the bank's branches in Paris and elsewhere were limiting payment in silver to 600 francs. Larger payments had to be made in gold or notes. Most people preferred the convenience of the latter. They assumed the paper money could be redeemed safely.

Initially, all went well. The bank lent money to the state and to private entrepreneurs. Business did revive and trade started to expand. One clear area for expansion was the New Colonies, but an investment scheme directed at Louisiana in North America was to become a controversial and tragic failure.

Historical connection 8

Though the Spanish were the first Europeans to enter the territory on the southern coast of North America that was to be Louisiana, France won the three-nation race to claim and settle the area. This supremacy over England and Spain was gained initially by the actions of Robert Cavalier, Sieur de la Salle. He explored the drainage basin of the Mississippi, claimed the area for France and named it in honour of King Louis XIV. Later, two Canadian explorers, the Moyne brothers, established a fort and settlement at New Biloxi on the Gulf of Mexico. By March 1699, there were around 200 people here. However, it was a demanding life and those surviving the initial rigours of this new frontier moved upstream around 1714 to establish a more permanent settlement at Natchitoches.

Early trading and development was in the hands of Antoine Crozat, a financier. On 24th

September 1712, King Louis XIV granted Crozat the exclusive right to trade in Louisiana for fifteen years. The initial commercial interest centred on the exploitation of the potential mineral wealth.

Other settlements began to appear. A permanent European settlement was in place in 1715 at a fort established by Louis St Denis and the first slaves were brought to the territory in June 1716. In 1717, Crozat sold his rights to John Law and this transaction inaugurated the Mississippi Scheme.

By 1718, Governor Bienville, named a new settlement at the mouth of the Mississippi River in honour of the Regent of France, Philippe, duc of Orléans.

New Orleans, Nov. 1718

Bienville has instructed his engineering staff to lay out streets for the town, although there are now only 68 inhabitants. Bienville is hoping to make New Orleans the capital of Louisiana, replacing the Gulf Coast town of Biloxi.[25]

It was not long before 'New Orleans' had replaced Biloxi as the most important centre in Louisiana. Initially, only French settlers were welcome in the new territory and many of these did not go by choice.

To establish the credit his 'system' required to succeed, Law bent his peculiar genius to attract money and people to the Mississippi valley, describing the 'almost incredible advantages' of the landed concession, shares in which he peddled throughout Europe as well as in France. New Biloxi...was to serve as a trans-shipping point for vast inland developments (the exploitation of mountains of precious metals and stones – gold diamonds, emeralds – was part of the plan; Indians bedecked with gold were paraded through Paris) that would definitely and finally secure the prosperity of French empire. Lacking voluntary colonists to Louisiana, the government sent foundlings, vagabonds, criminals and prostitutes.[26]

Most of these particular settlers had neither the skills for agriculture nor the necessary predispositions needed for successful farming. By December 1719, the territory was accepting other Europeans. Most of these were fleeing the turmoil from the wars created by Louis XIV. They included German farmers and peasants who because they could contribute to the enhancement of food production were regarded by Law as *'just the kind of colonists we need'*.[27] By 1728, *filles à la cassette* or 'casket girls' chaperoned by Ursuline nuns were arriving in New Orleans. They were named after the small chests carrying their trousseaux. The girls, mostly in their teens, were educated and from middle-class families judged to have provided them with 'good character' and healthy bodies. They were sent to marry the wealthier colonists and so hopefully bring more respect and family stability to the now established port and its surrounding lands.

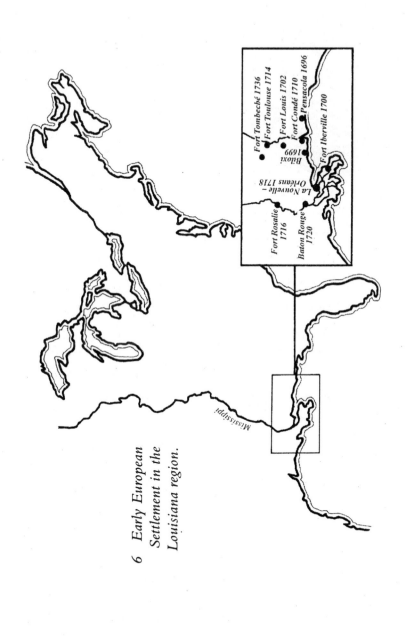

6 *Early European*
   Settlement in the
   Louisiana region.

Fort Tombecbé 1736
Fort Toulouse 1714
Fort Louis 1702
Fort Condé 1710
Pensacola 1696
Biloxi 1699
Fort Iberville 1700
La Nouvelle – Orléans 1718
Fort Rosalie 1716
Baton Rouge 1720

Mississippi

Finance to Flight

LAW BECAME most actively associated with the development of this territory through his 'Compagnie d'Occident ou de la Louisiana', better known as the Mississippi Company. This company was set up in August 1717 and within a short space of time it enjoyed exclusive privileges. These included the opportunity to colonise and develop commercially the vast area of the Mississippi valley. The shares issued were eagerly absorbed and initially the company expanded rapidly. In 1718, it acquired a monopoly over the production and distribution of tobacco. In the same year it absorbed the Senegal Company and bought control of the French mint. In 1719 Law and his business associates bought up the East India Company. The Company was then offered a fifty-year extension on its privileges and in return it accepted the right of farming all indirect taxes. The company also lent the French government around 1,500 millions at a loan rate of three per cent. This loan was urgently needed to pay off accumulated debt. However, those seeking to take their credit had to accept company shares at the current price.

Throughout 1719 Law's system was thriving and his company, now known as 'La Compagnie des Indes', was at the height of popularity. The value of the initial shares rose significantly and set in motion a wave of speculation. Though the specific figures attached to the shares during this period of investor excitement vary from historical source to historical source, the first shares jumped to a height of about thirty-five times their initial value before becoming more static at about nineteen times the initial cost.

At this successful time, Law was also accepting government bills and thereby making a contribution to reducing the national debt. By early 1720 he had become very eminent in France. He chose to put aside his protestant faith and turned to Catholicism. The motives for doing this may have been genuine conversion of some kind, but, commercially speaking, he would not have forgotten that when an earlier financial plan of his had been put to Louis XIV, *the bigoted monarch wished to know if Law was a Catholic*. On being informed that he was not *he refused to inquire into the merits of the case declaring that he would have nothing to do with a heretic.*[1]

During January 1720, the vigorous, some say ruthless, sales campaign to exploit the economic potential of Louisiana continued. Investors could not get into the scheme fast enough and when the Companie issued a forty per cent dividend the share price rose well above the capital base to sustain it.

This risk was not in the consciousness of those infatuated with the Mississippi project. Eager applicants besieged Law in the rue Quincampoix and some took adjacent apartments to press their claim and monitor its progress. However, as with all inflationary episodes, some local characters prospered. Anecdote holds that some houses in adjacent streets trebled in price and some who woke poor in the morning went to bed with riches.

7   *The vibrant rue Quincampoix at the time of the 'system'.*

As the desire to invest reached fever pitch, speculation outstripped prudence. By February 1720, a number of factors interlocked and turned the tide very strongly against John Law. The esteem attached to his character, his socially influential prowess and his rich and varied financial interests went into rapid decline.

First, La Compagnie des Indes amalgamated with the Banque Royale, and in a society with no experience of global multinationals and where travel and communication was relatively slow and very risky, the size of this modest commercial group probably alarmed some speculators. Perhaps they drew an analogy with a bubble, getting ever larger until inevitably it would burst. Certainly in later lampooning of Law, balloon imagery and the notion of a windbag figure significantly.

Second, Law's growing popularity and eminence in France had brought him enemies. He contested not only with commercial volatility but also with political intrigue and open envy. The latter was in no small measure connected with the high regard in which French ladies held him. Their eagerness either to sight Law, or be in proximity to him, is euphemistically portrayed in a reply said to be given on the matter to the Regent. He, being desirous of a Duchess to attend upon his daughter, stated that unfortunately, "I do not know where to find one." A respondent intimated, "You have only to go to Mr Law's; you will see everyone in his ante-chamber."[2]

Third, Law had never secured the full support of the French *Parlement*. During 1718 those members more virulently opposed to Law's schemes had proposed he should face trial for interference in the finances of the state. A few went as far as suggesting he should face capital punishment if found guilty.

...it was the Parlement that served as the initiator, if not actually the instigator of the riots over John Law in 1720.[3]

Law went to the Palais Royal under the protection of the Regent and after the imprisonment of some key parliamentary figures; greater obedience was secured from the sceptics. The obedience was not, however, long-lasting, largely because several in *Parlement* had grave misgivings about the delicate framework upon which the State's finances rested. These concerns grew in strength when it appeared that the Royal Bank was issuing paper notes on the basis of fabrication rather than a secure financial foundation. The increase in the circulation of paper money became exponential, though it appears that the flood occurred after the bank passed from direct management by John Law himself.

Finally, the debacle was probably hastened by an influence that affects all trading markets, insecurity compounded by rumour. Especially where an individual's money or that from a social or business circle is at stake, it is often the case that fanciful argument is allowed to outweigh economic reasoning. The bourgeois speculators of the period were nervous on many counts and a good number of them got into the scheme more from the motive of greed than entrepreneur activity on behalf of the state. They were probably 'looking over their shoulder' from the beginning for any risk likely to attach itself to their fortune. The nervousness could be utilised by those siding against Law, especially the bankers, tax farmers and investment treasurers whose earlier monopoly of the market had been swept aside by his system. As the speculation grew in intensity, strongly fuelled by the initial high dividend, those opposed to Law were active in explaining how the commercial developments of the Company could not possibly have the reserves and prospects to sustain the level of return.

> At this point the opposition of treasurers, tax farmers and bankers whose monopolies were threatened by the interloper became significant; it was easy for them to point out that the commercial companies could not show profits or prospects remarkable enough to justify the weight of credit mounted on them.[4]

These four influences probably combined to set in motion an unstoppable and irreversible trend of events. The inflationary process had gained too much momentum and it is possible that both the Regent and John Law had lost sight of an earlier Law maxim that *a banker deserved death who made issues of paper without the necessary funds to provide for them.* Everything was set to fall apart.

> All went reasonably well, until greed – or prescience – persuaded the Prince de Conti to

arrive, on 2 March, with three covered wagons, demanding gold from the bank in exchange for fourteen million shares. The following day, another eminent aristocrat, the Duc de Conde-Bourbon, a prince of the blood no less, rolled up insisting that he sell twenty-five million shares. The Regent was appalled: 'It appears Monsieur, that you take pleasure in destroying in a moment that which we have had so much trouble in establishing.... What are you going to do with such a great amount of money?'[5]

It is said that the action of the Prince de Conti arose from Law denying him more shares in India stock and at his own price. Under pressure from the Regent, de Conti did refund the bank two-thirds of his withdrawal but the die was cast. Although it took a little longer than a 'moment' to destroy Law's system, the end came within a few months. Those wanting to exchange or sell, far outstripped any speculators wanting to invest. A drastic devaluation was inevitable. The reduced value was announced in a notice issued on 21st May 1720. This stated that the value of the bank notes was to be gradually reduced to one half. Panic ensued, possibly inflamed by *Parlement's* refusal to enact the requirement, and vacillation around what value the notes would have. Just one week later the bank suspended all payment.

—the notes lost all credit, none would meddle with them; and the avenues of the bank being blocked up by soldiers there was no possibility of getting near the tellers, so that…one might have starved with 100 millions of paper money in his pocket.[6]

The foundation of the 'Mississippi Scheme' was a system of credit. The nature of the credit had initially evolved to extricate the French from the enormous state debt, but the credit had also underpinned colonisation and commercial expansion overseas. Law still felt there was sufficient scope to retrieve some of the tremendous loss and his reorganisation of the constituent companies that comprised the Compagnie des Indes did put in place a platform that helped overseas trade to stabilise and revitalise in the decades before the French Revolution.

However, he could not immediately restore the value of the paper money and eventually the Regent withdrew the paper from circulation. As with all investments, a few had made huge fortunes by selling at the right time, but many had lost and several others had been ruined. The popular description became *every rich man thought himself ruined without resource, and every poor man saw himself a beggar.*[7] Anger escalated, discontent became openly manifest and eventually aggressive social discourse turned into social disharmony and civil disorder. Some people were crushed to death as everyone sought to get into the banks to retrieve what they could. Law himself and his wife and daughter narrowly escaped the clutches of the now familiar mob, but others were less fortunate. Murder and robbery became somewhat commonplace as some sought to survive and others to re-establish their fortune and status. The Parisians renamed their Monsieur Lass. He became Monsieur Helas (Mr Alas!).

Initially, the Regent stood firm in the face of parliamentary disquiet and public disorder and even kept faith with Law by allowing him presence in the royal box at the opera. However, he also took steps to appease his opponents. Law was removed from office (*Contrôleur général* of French finance) and was now only admitted to the Palais Royal at night or through clandestine arrangements. The man whom the Duke of Orléans had become accustomed to consulting upon every matter of the moment and who had been almost worshipped by a section of the French community slipped to living in his house with a detachment of Swiss Guards. He took steps not to reveal his identity in the streets and always travelled further afield incognito. When even the detachment of guards could not make his home secure, the Regent allowed him to retreat to the Palais Royal. Despite Law's best effort in the months that followed, his whole system was soon to be demolished.

Historical connection 9

Between 1711 and 1720, the British also managed to put in place a disastrous trading scheme based on overseas investment. A trading venture known as the South Sea Company was established in 1711. Initially, the focus of the trade was the transportation of slaves to Spanish America. From this unfortunate, but at the time not illegal base, the Company expanded into other trading enterprises. As with the *Compagnie d'Occident* at first all went well. The early successes lead to vibrant speculation in the Company's shares. Investors clamoured to get on board and at the peak of trading shares were changing hands at ten times their initial value. Unfortunately, few of the investors were aware that the scheme included many subsidiary companies that were worthless.

Like its French counterpart, the South Sea Company offered in 1720 to take over thirty million of the national debt. They would do this by giving government creditors South Sea stock in exchange for their annuity holdings. The offer was made very attractive, since these annuities already paid reasonable interest until the year of the holder's death. The transfer of the annuities would provide five per cent per annum until 1727 and four per cent from then on.

Parliament's acceptance of the proposal was speedy and given without a definite statement on what value of South Seas stock would be exchanged for government annuities. This lack of open declaration checked restraint and may have encouraged the company to push up the price of stock. The government's embrace of the company's proposal to take over some of the nation's debt, followed by further rounds of volatile trading, led to a wild increase in the value of the shares. By September 1720, however, they had found their true level and a slump arrived. The shares soon became worthless and the 'burst' of the South Sea bubble ruined many investors.

They agitated for explanation and justice. Gross fraud was soon apparent for the Company had nothing like the level of trading that had been claimed. Some high-ranking individuals at the king's court were implicated in the corruption and members of the government had been bribed to declare that the company was healthy. Those ruined agitated to a point where the exposed scandal seemed to threaten the crown and the government.

Sir Robert Walpole became the man for the day.

He took control of the crisis and worked to put a recovery plan in place. Taking an idea proposed by his own investment manager and banker, Robert Jacombe, he proposed that the Bank of England and the East India Company should take over the shares so that some of the investors could receive a level of repayment.[8]

> This he did by persuading both the bank of England and the East India Company to take 9 million each of South Sea Stock, thus ending the free fall in its value. By the end of the year it was up to 200 (from 190) a sure sign of returning confidence. The transferees received between 60 per cent and 80 per cent of the original sums.[9]

This measure took the eye from the storm and some accompanying 'spin' of the day glossed over the government's part in the deception. Unfortunately John Law did not have someone of the stature of Walpole to intervene in his calamity.

The South Sea Company continued trading until 1865 but the Bubble Act passed in 1720 restricted the formation of the type of joint trading that had led to the initial deception.

The simultaneous collapse in Britain and France of two large-scale investment schemes severely reduced confidence in paper money, credit schemes and the conduct of public and private finance. It strengthened the Bank of England's position but it was to be eighty years before France would have another national bank.

In France the long-term damage was more psychological than material. There were two principal effects. First, the *memory of it inhibited most future attempts in France at radical financial restructuring.*[10] Second, for many years the term 'credit' was preferred to 'banque' to the point were the two descriptions are now both equally present in the titles of French banks. Ironically, the one thing that did hold its value following the collapse of the Banque Royale was land.

Though he didn't know at the time, the South Sea escapade was to catch up with John Law in 1721.

Debacle to Death

My shares which on Monday I bought.
Were worth millions on Tuesday, I thought.
So on Wednesday I chose my abode;
In my carriage on Thursday I rode;
To the ball-room on Friday I went;
To the workhouse next day I was sent.[1]

DESPITE WIDESPREAD and continuing hostility towards him, Law struggled on attempting to sort out the debacle that had seen company shares fall rapidly by fifty per cent. Despite his courage and resolve, it was almost inevitable he would not succeed. First, his financial reputation and influence were in shreds. Second, following the burst of the 'bubble', no one believed any longer that shares of stock could be regarded as identical to money. Third, the collapse resulted in volatile inflation, and the price of many things changed almost by the hour. Fourth, those who had always opposed him, including many members of the *Parlement* in Paris, hastened his demise. Finally, the Regent himself was no longer absolutely secure and although he did support Law's re-emergence for a time under the title *'conseiller d'épée et intendant général du commerce'* and agreed to let him visit Fresnes to discuss a rescue plan with the former Chancellor (D'Aguesseau), the 'system' was by now beyond reclaim. This meant that Philippe himself came more directly under attack.

> When a deputation from parlement complained to him about the lack of currency, he promised he would see to it, but when asked when that might be, he snapped, 'Ah, when, when, when, I do not know; When I can!' The irritability was brought on by his awareness that the revocation of the edict of 21 May, the return of D'Aguesseau, all other measures he had taken, were failing to restore calm or confidence. D'Aguesseau hurried between the Palais-Royal and the Ile de la Cite trying to keep a dialogue going with parlement. But by this stage parlement wanted only one thing, the departure of John Law.[2]

Inevitably the Regent, supported by the Duke of Bourbon, suggested to Law the expediency of his leaving the city and the country. They offered him financial assistance, since his property had been confiscated and his personal fortune of around ten million livres was now reduced to about 800. Law prepared to go but said he would do so with his own limited funds.

It was not easy for Philippe to abandon Law. He had been an early and firm protagonist for the 'system' and could not carry through a volte-face without some loss of personal credibility. He had also seen a significant reduction in the national debt through Law's acceptance of government bills as collateral to purchase shares in the Mississippi Company. Ironically, even though the bank was in decline, the *Compagnie des Indes* stayed commercially active and Philippe was also receiving positive indications from priests and explorers about the potential for agricultural development and other commercial ventures in Louisiana.

Three influences combined to underpin his acceptance of Law going into exile. First, civil disobedience was becoming continuous. It was costing lives and significant damage to property. Second, Law's growing authoritarian attempts at remediation seemed to be making the civil strife worse – more especially the introduction of a passport to leave the country and unwelcome intrusions through 'searches' into the financial and domestic status of those who retained some wealth. Third, and perhaps most influential, Cardinal Dubois saw in Law's fall an opportunity to reconcile the Regent and the *Parlement* while at the same time saving the Regent from going down with Law. At the end of the day, both Philippe and the Cardinal seemed to have concluded that the only real and pragmatic option was to offer the head of Law to his most ardent enemies.

Towards the end of 1720, private financiers took back the reigns of French finance. From the outset of his proposals, many of these agents had done their best to disgrace Law. They saw a loss of lucrative business to a reliable banking system. Now with the central agency of finance, the royal bank, insecure and unappealing, they once again had control over annuities, loans and commercial investment. The return to prominence of these financiers and their aristocratic underwriters put the French financial structure almost back to where it had been under the *Ancien Régime*.

> Their good business was France's bad. The raising of taxes, servicing of loans, were more wasteful and expensive. Interest rates were higher because there was no attractive, secure, central agency of investment. ... Law's opponents were shortsighted, even in terms of their own financial interests.[3]

Even if France's financial structure had been reversed and made worse, the love affair between the French and John Law was well and truly over. He left the country secretly in December 1720. In effect he was disgraced and for all intents and purposes banished by the *Parlement*. At the time of his departure, the fact that he was not alone in setting up the failed financial ventures seemed overlooked. He left believing he would be recalled.

His belief that he would once again find favour and further fortune in France is underwritten by the fact that initially he only went about forty miles to an estate he owned east of Paris. The estate of Guermande had been acquired during his more prosperous days. Though said to include a fine house with graceful grounds, it had been used principally only by his son John and a few members of the extended family. Law thought he would wait at Guermande until the financial affairs of the bank and company had been cleared up. He was mistaken. Within a few days former friends and business acquaintances arrived. They were acting on behalf of the Regent. They brought passports in two names and some gold to wish him *bon voyage* and to help him move on. They suggested he make for Rome, but Law now conscious that his son was showing a tendency to practise his own precocious teenage ways, thought the city might be too much of a temptation for the seventeen-year-old. He left with the passports but again refused the financial help. He made his way with the younger John to the Netherlands.

He was recognised at the Netherlands frontier and delayed for forty-eight hours until a letter from the Regent freed them to proceed. The personal wealth that the senior John had brought out (around 800 gold louis) was confiscated by the district *Intendant* who reminded Law that it had been he who had instituted the mandate restricting the export of specie. The *Intendant* claimed that he had delayed Law out of fear to let such a notorious figure pass without higher authority, but his action and the confiscation of Law's survival funds seemed equally motivated by the *Intendant's* chance to repay Law for the financial actions that had removed his own father from a lucrative office.

In the years immediately after 1720, Law was as restless as he had been before assuming his unique status in France. His wandering was now more by circumstance than choice. The loss of his residual wealth meant he had initially to seek out those friends and acquaintances that still respected him and therefore would offer some level of support. He also retained a passion still to prove himself in relation to banks and credit systems and he thus sought audiences with those in high places who might have an interest in resurrecting his core idea, albeit in modified form.

He arrived in Brussels on 22nd December 1720 and was received hospitably by the governor. Various members of the local nobility also helped him financially. He asked the French Minister in Brussels to try to retrieve the funds taken from him at the border. When news reached him that some of the principal figures in the Royal Bank were now in the Bastille and that some of those who believed he owed them recompense were already in pursuit of him, he considered it wise to move further from France. On Christmas Day he wrote to the Duke of Bourbon:

I left Brussels yesterday evening and, although the roads are very bad, I propose to continue my journey to Italy. The Regent has expressed the desire that I should retire to Rome; that determines me. The enemies of the system have taken umbrage at seeing me within reach of France and have been seeking to cause me trouble, although I am outside the Kingdom. It will cost me nothing to satisfy them. I have always hated work. A hope well founded on doing good to people and being of service to the prince who had given me his confidence – these were the ideas which inspired and sustained me throughout an unpleasant business. I have now returned to my natural self.'[4]

By January 1721 his party had reached Venice, and he was active in this city under the nomenclature of his second passport, M du Jardin. Father and son found the Venetian context both pleasant and relatively safe. The autocratic government policed essentially only those internal and external incumbents perceived to be a political threat. The city was vigorously into its licentious days of masques, incognito balls and loose morals. Gambling flourished.

Gaming halls were more patronised than its theatres – both of them generally belonged to noblemen. Some of these owners spent day and night at the tables running the games; the most famous of these the Ridotto at San Moisé had ten gaming rooms. Less dangerous were the Caffes: the famous Florian and Quadri in Piazza San Marco were inaugurated in 1720 and in 1745.[5]

8   *Florians in Venice.*

In general there was a high degree of tolerance of characters seen to be a little secret and socially intriguing. Despite the fact that the 'du Jardin' mask was quickly demolished and Law's true identity was widely known in the city, he seemed to feel secure enough to stay until the end of the lengthy carnival period. At the close of this

festival period his resolution was to move on to Rome. He was still clinging on to the hope of revised fortunes.

Law never did make the city founded by Romulus. Though he set out with his son in March 1721, he heard en route that his creditors planned to seek restorative justice through attaching their claims to a prominent indigenous Roman citizen. This meant he was liable for arrest in that part of Italy. He retreated back to Venice.

The general congeniality of Venetian lifestyle suited Law and this, coupled with the fatigue of recent travel, the need for daily survival and his growing disappointment, seems to have curbed any desire for further recognition and advancement through financial ventures. He turned down an offer to go to Copenhagen to help put Danish finances into better shape, pleading his lack of stamina to cope with their climate and his desire now to lead only a tranquil life. In the summer of 1721 he also deferred an offer from the Tsar Peter the Great to introduce the 'system' into Russia. He would be aware of the Tsar's growing unpopularity with several European nations as a result of his actions in the Baltic; the climate would have suited him less well than that in Denmark, and catastrophic failure in Russia would almost certainly lead to a harsh term of imprisonment.

He did not though expect to be alone in Venice for a calm and contented life. His wife Katherine was still in Paris and he wrote to her in April 1721 saying that although he liked Venice very much he did not intend to be there always. He was also desirous of having

Katherine's company again, either by being given permission to return to Paris on a temporary basis, or having her join him in exile. Letters from both of them to the Regent failed to advance their cause. For Katherine and her daughter life in the French capital could not have been easy.

> Madame Law is again to be seen in Paris...and she cuts a striking figure with her daughter, but she is surrounded by creditors.[6]

His wife's position, plus the growing realisation that a return to wealth and proper status in France was unlikely, propelled Law in two directions. He spent more time gambling where he used his formidable powers of the laws of probability to tempt the less mathematically astute to risk wagers on very unlikely odds. He also sought to set in motion a return to London, since he hoped he might have a better chance there of settling many unresolved financial affairs.

Historical connection 10

When asked the question 'If you had it all to do over, would you change anything?' Winston Churchill replied, 'Yes I wish I had played the black instead of the red at Cannes and Monte Carlo.' The reply illustrates the fascination most

---

of us have with games of chance, the element of risk and the rules of probability. It also indicates that most of us have to settle on losing rather than winning.

The dream of 'beating the odds' is well established in the human psyche, as is the perception that many aspects of our lives are something of a gamble. Well before John Law used the rules of chance and guile to help him maintain a living, very able and not so able minds have pondered on risk versus potential outcomes. Games of chance were in existence some 3000 years BC and the anklebones from cloven-hoofed animals were one of the earliest forms of dice. Over the centuries chance has been used to relieve boredom, to choose courses of action, to settle debts of honour and to simulate potential risk.

The most popular games of chance in Law's time were faro and basset. Faro dates from around the fifteenth century and the name given to the players ('punters') is one of the earliest recorded uses of this term. The suite of spades provides the host cards. These are placed in two rows – highest cards nearest the dealer, with the cards 1 to 6 forming the lower layout. The card number 7 is placed to the right of the two rows and sits between them as a kind of bridge.

Punters place wagers on one or more specific cards, or they hedge their bet by placing the wager midway between two cards or four cards. The dealer is in charge of the 'turns' – each 'turn' is a sequence of two cards – the first takes any winnings for the dealer, the second goes to the punters. For example, if the first card turned is a ten, the dealer collects all wagers placed on that, if the second card is a six, any wagers placed there are paid for by the dealer. The return is 'level' meaning that what is waged is won – 1 gets 1 back, 100 gets another 100. The turned cards are discarded and the game continues until the pack has been used. Punters may leave or join between turns and in these gaps they may also increase any wagers laid. This description is of the basic game and there were many variations. Faro became more prevalent when basset was under scrutiny.

The name 'basset' derives from the Italian 'Basetta'. A 'banker' takes charge of the game and lays down a sum of money to cover winning cards. Each punter has thirteen cards. One or

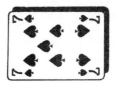

9   *The layout for the card game Faro.*

more cards are used to lay wagers. The banker, known as the *talliere* deals the first card (the *fasse*) and pays one half of any wagers laid on that number irrespective of suite. The second card turned wins for the punters. The next for the *talliere*. Thus for every two cards turned the call will be 'ace wins, ten loses', 'king wins, seven loses' and so on. When a punter wins they might choose to take the winnings or to turn the corner of the card indicating willingness to try for higher advantage. This was showing *paroli*. There were also other levels of temptation including 'double or quit' and 'masse' whereby more money might be staked on a card seen to be doing well.

Clearly the sum of money laid down by the banker had to be substantial if a number of players chose to place 'high stakes'. This was recognised by Louis XIV who decreed that only sons of noblemen or those with considerable fortunes should hold the role of *talliere*.

As the eighteenth century progressed, both games resulted in the loss or gain of huge fortunes. They were made illegal in both France and England to prevent members of the nobility becoming ruined and disgraced.

Faro was said to offer odds near to evens, but this relied upon fair playing conditions and to some extent on a player's capacity to remember the cards that had been taken from the pack. Basset is a kind of lottery – and as with modern versions *the success of those who organise gambling is some indication of the profits to be derived from the efficient use of chance.*[7]

John Law had the advantage of strong mathematical capacity.

The bent of his inclination, however, prompting him to apply, in a particular manner, to the studies of arithmetic and geometry, he made himself so complete a master of these branches as to be able to resolve with the utmost facility the most intricate problems in them; and it was remarked that none more perfectly understood the complex science of algebra.[8]

—he had a head fit for calculations of all kinds to an extent beyond anybody.[9]

He also had the advantage of understanding the rules of probability and years of experience of studying 'the odds' in various gaming houses over Europe. He often took on what many even today consider too risky, the role of 'banker' or *talliere*, yet it is clear that even in the basic version of these games, those arranging to pay have a prodigious advantage over those laying the wager. John Law knew that the people who gambled with him had a relatively small probability of winning, and he would certainly not have told them – 'you might win a "tenner", but you probably won't win the jackpot.'

Though throughout most of his life Law was an ardent 'professional gambler', something akin to the bookmakers of today, he was not in general a supporter of state lotteries. In 1726 he made it clear that such lotteries invoked a spirit of distorted self-indulgence. He suggested – *wealth should be acquired by industry, and not by luck or gaming.*[9] Perhaps he viewed his later renewed efforts at the Ridotto in Venice as an industrious match of intellectual skills with the rules of probability, not an indulgent dream based on chance randomisation.

Law did reach London but by circuitous means. He visited Copenhagen in October 1721 and at that time knew that his request to return to England had been approved. There was a strong naval presence in Copenhagen when he arrived. It was there to stand protection for Sweden against any expansion plans by the Tsar. When tension eased and with the likelihood of little aggression by sea over the forthcoming winter months, the British Fleet, under the command of Sir John Norris, prepared to put to sea for home shores.

Law and his son were granted passage by Norris and they arrived on English soil in late October. Law was met by business acquaintances, some there from loyalty, others to press concerns about non-payment of credit bills and losses incurred through the Mississippi venture. Unfortunately for Law, the English Parliament seemed to pick up from the point where the *Parlement* of Paris had been. There were questions about the purposes of him being in the country, the morality of this happening and the justification for him being there by right of passage in an English vessel. Earl Coningsby raised the most vociferous objections in the House of Lords. He spoke of disreputable past behaviour, the practice of mischief by Law in a neighbouring country, his dismissal of his own national status through taking French citizenship, his leanings towards Jacobitism and the cause of the Pretender, and gross contempt shown for his own religion by his turning to Catholicism.

More fortunate for Law, Coningsby was regarded by

many as uncouth and ill-informed. In contrast, the member who spoke in defence of John Law, Lord Carteret, was considered to be clever and politically courageous. He was thirty-one years of age at the time, had just returned himself from Sweden where he had been serving as ambassador extraordinary and was set to forward his political ambition. In setting out a case for John Law he declared:

> 'Mr Law had many years ago the misfortune to kill a gentleman in a duel; but that, having received the benefit of the King's clemency and the appeal lodged by the relations of the deceased being taken off, he was come over to plead His Majesty's most gracious pardon; that there was no law to keep an Englishman out of his own country; and, as Mr Law was a subject of Great Britain, it was not even in the King's power to hinder him from coming home if he thought fit.'[11]

Law's Jacobite connections may have been intermittent and opportunist, as opposed to passionate advocacy,[12] but the fact that many saw him as having leanings to the Stuart cause and the fact that Coningsby had made open reference to it, makes Carteret's defence somewhat surprising. His own disposition was firmly that of a Tory who supported the house of Hanover. In 1715 he had shown that support by going to Cornwall

10 Lord Carteret.

to root out Jacobite traitors. This action contributed to his cousin, Lord Lansdowne, going to the Tower. It may be that he was persuaded of merits in Law's case by such people as the Duke of Argyll, who though a supporter of Law, was strongly against the Pretender's cause.

Whatever his motivation, Carteret's statement in the House of Lords was most helpful to Law. It reaffirmed that he had been notified earlier of the diminution of his original offence and given a discharge by Wilson's relatives regarding the unfortunate incident. The statement was of further help since, in an age where instant or speedy copying was not possible, he held no documentary proof of the situation outlined by

Carteret because most of his official papers were still in France.

Shortly after Carteret's stalwart declaration, John Law did attend before the King's Bench to plead his pardon. This was a formality because Law had already received written pardon three years earlier. King George I had sent this to him in France.

George I received Law for granting the pardon and must have been pleased to receive some non-political and non-regal contact in London who could speak French and some German, even if somewhat falteringly. George could hardly speak a word of English and took little interest in the English language and the social context of England.

> To contemporaries George seemed a distant figure. Unlike William III of Orange, who had seized power in 1688-89 and who was familiar with English politics and politicians from earlier visits, marriage into the English royal family and extensive intervention in English domestic politics, George knew relatively little of England and his first experience of it was as an older man than was the case with William (or James I).

> George's failure to learn English and his obvious preference for Hanover further contributed to this sense of alien rule. It caused considerable

complaint, among Whigs as well as Tories. Lady Anne Paulet was ready to believe a report that George would not return to Britain from Hanover for the winter of 1716-17 'for I fancy he is so much easier where he is that he will like to be from us as long as he can'. This concern was exacerbated by a sense that the preference for Hanover entailed an abandonment of British national interests...[13]

If Law thought that the audience with the King and his ceremonial appearance at Westminster Hall were steps to lead back to wealth, status and honour, he was mistaken. Though his stay in England was to span the next three years, he was further troubled throughout this time.

The first difficulty was that the burst of the South Sea Company rebounded on him. Inevitably, Law became linked in the minds of the credulous public with the South Sea collapse. He was quickly identified as the true author of economic ruin and the main culprit for the arising misfortunes. He was accused of promoting a system that was not substantial and which had lead to other imitations that were equally unsound. As in France, he became the butt for disquiet and ill-will.

I have found the public very prejudiced against me, even some of the first in the land. The losses they have suffered in the South Sea Company have so distorted their judgement that they no longer listen to reason. I find myself condemned without being heard, while bad luck is represented as a crime. I am regarded as the author of their evils, on the ground that the system which I established in France led England to embark upon the South Sea venture.[14]

Law's second problem was lack of funds. This restricted the standard of his living but more importantly it reduced the opportunities he had to mix in high society and to gamble at the level he was used to. It also meant that creditors regularly pressed him. They either wanted settlement for links with French investment, or they would not advance goods and services as they did for others, for fear of non-payment. Some friends did help him, including the compassionate, though ill-regarded mistress of the Prince of Wales, Mrs Henrietta Howard. Clearly their help was insufficient to meet Law's needs and some correspondence with Mrs Howard shows him to be in something of a desperate state.

Can you not prevail on the Duke to help me something more than the half year? Or is there nobody that could have the good nature enough to lend me one thousand pounds? I beg that, if nothing of this can be done, it may only be betwixt us two, as I take you as my great friend...[15]

That Henrietta tried to help Law indicates the esteem she must have attached to him and the regard she held for his immediate and loyal circle of friends. Certainly on the commercial side she had no reason to thank him. On the advice of the Campbell brothers (second Duke of Argyll and the Earl of Ilay) she had invested in the Mississippi scheme. Financially speaking, she may also have been unfortunate on a second front, for one of the large settlements made on her behalf by the Prince of Wales was £11,500 worth of stock in the South Sea Company. Perhaps more negatively, from Law's point of view, but he probably didn't know it, though she was the prince's mistress, her personal, social and political influence on him then and later as king (George II) was not significant. He:

> seemed to look upon a mistress rather as a necessary appurtenance to his grandeur as a prince than as an addition to his pleasures as a man.[16]

Despite Henrietta's strong qualities, including those of wit, a sense of calm, coping with her deafness without fuss and attracting to her men of strong intellect, Law may have expected too much from her relationship with the prince. It was the routine sort of affair not uncommon in European courts of the day.

> It was…an unusual and apparently not a very passionate affair, one to which she had to

submit in order to remain at Court, and of which the Princess Caroline more or less approved.[17]

11   Henrietta Howard.

Henrietta did secure small royal bequests for Law and he was, no doubt, grateful. She was eventually to free herself from a very unhappy marriage and, after her affair with the prince ended, who was by then king, she found her own status by investing time in the design and development of the Palladian villa Marble Hill. She also made a second more happy marriage and retained a close circle of intellectual friends.

Law was not to be so lucky. Back in France, problems were compounding for him. On leaving the country he had given Katherine power of attorney over his papers and his business affairs. They were not legally married and the fact that she was not his 'wife in standing' was now used to invalid her power of attorney. It was also made public that the children were 'bastards' and that in eyes of the law they had no existence. The rest of his family were still denied permission to leave France and his brother William had now been imprisoned there.

Though his intellectual capacity was as sharp as ever and he began to write a history of his experience, and a separate paper comparing the Mississippi and South Sea schemes, his physical health was not as good as it had been and this was being further affected by his reduced circumstances. He only survived the severe winter of 1722-23 by selling a few of his significantly reduced possessions and by cash handouts, including a sum of money sent by King George I.

He may have gone further down at this point, but for a surprising turn of events in the spring of 1723. The Regent granted him a retrospective pension and his brother was released from prison. He was also allowed to sell his library in Paris and some other possessions for small sums. His overtures to Paris to be recalled for service and his approaches to Robert Walpole for work on behalf of the English state seemed to intertwine into a durable thread. On hearing that Law might be recalled to Paris, Walpole saw that he might be useful for sustaining Anglo-French relations. In Walpole's mind it was a touch of 'better the devil you know than the one you don't'. He knew that the existing French protagonist for *entente cordial*, Cardinal Dubois was about to undergo an operation that few at the time survived. He thus wrote to the embassy in Paris:

> ...there can be no doubt that the power might fall into worse hands; and if any who are neither Englishmen by birth or affection should prevail, we should have less chance then by admitting one who has sundry ties to wish well his native country.[18]

Dubois did not make it through the operation and a fatigued and rather enfeebled Regent took control of still more state affairs. Law began to think his return was possible and prepared to go over the Channel. Unfortunately, fate was preparing to deal him his worst hand. On 2nd December 1723, the Duke of Orléans was with his mistress in an apartment at the Palais Royal. It was said that they were engaged in jest about the reality of God, and the actuality of heaven and hell. Though he was only forty-nine years old, the Regent's excesses interrupted the debate. He said he was becoming unwell; he fell forward and died within a few moments in the arms of the Duchess of Falaris. Law had lost his most influential contact in France and the one Frenchman who fully understood the potential of his financial scheme.

Worse was to come. He lost his pension, which the Regent had arranged to be sent to him. Rumours continued to circulate in France and England that as the 'system' was collapsing he had sent huge sums of money out of France and was waiting to use these funds in the near future. Though he wrote a series of logically ordered letters to debunk this myth and to make claim to the just reserves he had left behind, the false accusation did not end and finally he addressed his frustration to King Louis XV:

> If I only had the half of what I brought into France, Your Royal Highness would not be troubled today with my complaints.[19]

In truth Law was desperate to be able to arrange some recompense from France for he had no substantial assets in England or Scotland. By now, Lauriston was serving as security for various members of the wider family and even the minor level of gambling to which he was able to secure entry was not working in his favour.

The French continued to deny him. He was not allowed to go back to France and his wife Katherine, his daughter Mary Catherine, and his brother William were prevented from leaving Paris. Despite increasing bouts of ill-health and advancing age, he looked to find gainful employment. He was only fifty-three, but that was quite old for the time and his lifestyle, this underwritten by the Duc d' Orléans death at only forty-nine.

Since no Roman Catholic could benefit from a Crown post in 1742, not surprisingly his earlier conversion to Catholicism now worked against him. In truth, he was also something of an embarrassment to English ministers. Many in Parliament still disagreed with his presence in the country and the general public continued to have misgivings about his financial schemes. Work in Europe, but outside France, seemed the obvious answer. Law was to become an emissary overseas in the guise of a traveller on a journey to better his personal health. Robert Walpole offered him a commission in Munich as part of the strategy to restrict Austrian influence. In effect, the former Controller-General of France was beginning a new career as a secret agent or spy.

Historical connection 11

If selling sex is the oldest business in the world, being paid to spy must be nearly as old. Ancient rulers knew the value of getting reliable information about potential friends and enemies, and the role of being a 'scout' ahead of a main party often involved elements of espionage, as when Moses sent spies into the hill country of the Amorites so they could *'bring back a report about the route we are to take and the towns we will come to'.*[20]

Official secrecy encompasses a wide range of murky actions throughout a large part of British

---

and World history. The use of codes, double identities, infiltration and the spreading of false or malicious information have all featured in efforts to maintain facets of power or to defeat a real or potential enemy. The consequences of working as a secret agent or of assuming permanent or temporary allegiance with another nation to work against monarch or country have always been viewed as an extreme form of corruption. The High Treason Act dates to 1351 and was last amended in 1945. The Official Secrets Act began in formalised fashion in 1911 and was modified in 1989. Despite the Freedom of Information Act of 2000 (extended and refined in 2004) a culture of secrecy still pervades the British establishment and successive governments go to great lengths to restrict the release of potentially damaging information and to suppress embarrassing revelations.

Indeed, influential persons working on behalf of the crown have always initiated or supported spying and the use of secret service agents. For example, Francis Walsingham (1530-1590) supervised a network of spies to act in the best interests of Elizabeth I and to protect the country from a return to Catholicism.

The consequences of being caught in the act of passing on damaging information, being suspected of insurgency, acting as a spy, collaborator or conspirator, or committing an act of treason have always been severe. The histories of Mary Queen of Scots, Guy Fawkes, Walter Raleigh, John Andre, Edith Cavell, William Joyce (Lord Haw Haw) all attest to this. However, for the majority of people involved at the day-to-day level of secret information gathering, the work has tended to lack infamous reputation, high glamour and social intrigue. From the fifteenth century onwards, sons of the gentry who owed favours, undergraduates at Oxford and Cambridge, members of accepted ecclesiastical orders, and those like John Law, down on their luck, have all been recruited to collect scraps of information that might hold some significance. The roles of traveller or emissary were often used to send such people on secret missions abroad. Once there they had the dual task of supposedly acting for the purpose they had been allegedly sent, but in reality also acting surreptitiously as a government agent.

Most only engaged in relatively mundane, low-level 'spying' that was largely socially convenient.

They were often not privy to anything of substance – *I know that's a secret, for it's whispered everywhere.*[21] Their reports were often based on anecdote or unexpected conversations and often regarded by the powers of the day as transitory snippets that were largely ephemeral and of no consequence. They were kept in the field more in the hope they could one day justify their salary by being in the right place at the right time. In modern parlance they were more like 'sleepers' than active secret agents. The countries to which they were sent often easily deduced the real purpose for which they were present. They were tolerated or fed false information and just occasionally made an example of through imprisonment and torture.

John Law was no fool. Before commencing the journey to Munich he sought reassurance about his position and he requested some form of diplomatic identity or documentary protection. He was told accreditation letters would be prepared and sent on to him. These would give him official credence within the Republic of Venice. He was told to go to Aix-la-Chappelle (Aachen in Germany) and await further orders. He left London in August 1725. He did not come back to the city and he was never again to put his feet on English or Scottish soil.

Like Banff in Canada, the Matlocks in England, and Vichy in France, Aix-la-Chapelle had natural waters thought to have health benefits. In 1725, it acted as a 'spa town' for those seeking cures to all kinds of ailments. It was especially busy in the autumn and winter months, since in the decades before anti-inflammatory drugs appeared on the scene, those suffering arthritis, gout and rheumatism sought relief from their pain by bathing or resting in sulphur-based 'warm, organically enriched waters'. They also sought more than physical health routines and hence the town was a rich social scene. After taking the 'fashionable waters', the fashionable society moved on to partake of concerts, dancing or theatre. Law could once again move reasonably easily in such company, since Walpole had made sure that he received a regular salary by way of a local financier. However, he had been in similar and more grandiose social settings for much of his life and he quickly tired of the largely parochial Aachen circuit. He was anxious to do some work of merit, so much so that a letter back to Lord Townshend in England almost reads like a curriculum vitae and a potential job description. 'I am here awaiting His Majesty's orders.' He then outlines the locations with which he is familiar, the noble persons and families with whom he has had close contact, his time in French service and the influence he might still have, especially with the Bavarian Elector, Duke Maximilian Emmanuel. He concludes '…in the hope of being able to succeed in rendering good service to His Majesty.'

The reply merely confirmed Law's original orders. He was to proceed without further delay to Munich. He set out for the city but stays in Mannheim and Augsburg meant that Munich was not reached until 2nd January 1726, nearly four months after his departure from London. Even allowing for the trials and tribulations of travel at the time, the pace of his progress to Munich suggests that his 'secret mission' was not of the utmost importance.

Ill-fortune was still accompanying him. Duke Maximilian Emmanuel was not well and hence Law was received in his bedroom. The Bavarian Elector was still of the popular persuasion that Law had taken a personal fortune out of France and he pressed for help to reduce a high-interest debt. Law could only undertake to write to Sir Robert Walpole to ask for a loan from Britain to help meet the principality's obligations. The Elector never knew that Law's request was unsuccessful. He died just six weeks after Law's arrival and his successor, Duke Charles Albert, soon lost interest in Law when it became apparent that he was not able to secure substantial fiscal aid.

The honour in Law saw to it that he continued to serve his host nation dishonourably. He did this by carrying on with the 'spying' remit that lay at the base of his salary. He conscientiously sent back information to Whitehall but most of it was placed in the 'no action' file. Throughout 1726, Law was also being pressed uncomfortably for details of his 'system' by other rulers' emissaries. He responded in outline, but not detail, and he soon grew tired of further cross-examinations. This low point coincided with Whitehall's recognition that the changing Bavarian-Austrian scene meant that Law's location in Munich was of little use. His request at the end of 1726 to retire was granted. Almost six years after leaving Venice he arrived back at the waterborne city. By design or default, the timing was impressive – he was back for Carnival.

Perhaps within the psyche and biology of every person is the in-built clock that tells us the bell is tolling. Certainly for John Law he was pleased to be back in Venice and in his heart he was now there for the rest of his days. On the outward level, his life continued much as before – he gambled with some modicum of success and he finished the 1722 manuscript of his life and times in France. He coped better now with the constant stream of enquiries from those who believed his system had secret or even magical characteristics, and he spent time with interesting companions, including, it is said, the Chevalier de St George, father of Bonnie Prince Charlie, and the French philosophical historian Charles Louis de Secondat, Baron de la Brède et de Montesquieu.

Charles Louis was born at the Chateau de la Brède, near Bordeaux in 1689. He became counsellor of the *parlement* of Bordeaux in 1714 and its president in 1716. He was hard-working and had a strong inclination to pursue scientific enquiry. His fame, however, was to rest on literary success. In 1721 he published *Lettres persanes* (Persian letters), a satirical description of French society. In this work he had lampooned Law in allegoric style.

> In an island situated not far from the Orkneys there was born a child whose father was Eole, god of the winds, and whose mother was a nymph of Caledonia. It is said that he taught himself without any help to count on his fingers, and that from the age of four he was perfectly well able to distinguish the various metals that once, when his mother wished to give him a brass ring instead of a gold one, he recognised the deception and threw it in the ground.[22]

Montesquieu travelled widely, primarily to study political and social institutions. He spent much time in England during 1729-31, studying the writings of John Locke and analysing the English constitution. His best-known work *De l'espirit des lois* (*The Spirit of Laws*) was published in 1748. Through this work he has been attributed with presenting the idea of 'separation of powers' whereby state power has legislative, executive and judicial elements. This attribution may not be wholly correct, but his discussion of division of powers has '*entered into constitutional theory and constitution framing throughout the world*'.[23]

Though Law's meeting with Charles Louis did not lack civility, he was not able to persuade him of the merits of the system or project to him the best of his character. For Montesquieu described the inveterate but impoverished schemer as still dreaming of vast projects that would return him to power and France to prosperity.

> He is a captious man who must argue
> and the whole force of whose arguments
> is to attempt to turn your reply against
> you, by finding some objection in it.

> He was still the same man, with small
> means but playing high and boldly, his

mind occupied with projects, his head filled with calculations.[24]

Expressed as they are, these seem derogatory comments from a man regarded by himself and others as appreciating force of argument and the quest to search systematically for political and social doctrine. We do not know what Law thought of Charles Louis.

Whatever his outward appearance, on the inward level Law was aware that his energies were on the decline. This was hard to swallow for a man who from the beginning had tended to be self-reliant and who had formed numerous friendships but mainly of the transient kind. His wife and daughter remained in France and he was still pursued by those the system had failed and those who wanted to 'unlock the secret' of how to make debt vanish and wealth appear. Despite the fact that some people had done well by the 'system', Law himself in his very last years had no significant funds to help him cope with the rigours of old age. He probably drew solace from that fact that his son, the younger John, spent the exile years with him and that his wider family, though separated in distance from him, never renounced him or deserted him in spirit. He probably regretted his tendency at the height of his fame to soak up adulation and gratitude and to show little attention to those who stood in opposition to his wishes and aspirations. However, these personal characteristics are not uncommon in those who passionately espouse causes and those who achieve fame and public adoration.

Law was to see the Rialto Bridge for the last time on 25th February 1729. He was passing under the bridge as part of gondola tour when he become very cold and started with pronounced shivering. He was put to bed in his lodgings in the Piazza San Marco. He was never again to visit the canals and lagoons of his favoured city. Pneumonia set in and the end was imminent.

They give me fifteen days to live and I shall never find the time so long.[25]

I saw him for the last time the day before yesterday. He was then very sensible of the danger he was in and as he told me, very desirous to die, believing his death would be of greater service to his family at this juncture than any other, because the Cardinal {Fleury} has just now appointed three or four gentlemen to examine and state his accounts, and he thinks they will be more inclined to do him justice in France when they know how poor he dies and that he has nothing in any part of the world but in that country and in the King's hand.[26]

On 19th March 1729, Law was assisted in drawing

up a gift deed. In this bequest, 'from the residence of the most excellent John Law on St Mark's Square in the parish of San Gemigniano', he donated all his possessions to 'Milady Cattrina Knowel', sister of the Earl of Banbury, the said lady residing at present in Paris in her house situated in the Place Louis-le-Grand. This was his common-law wife Madame Law, though the 'state of his affairs required it so' that he did not formally execute the bequest in favour of her in that title.

He shared the dawn of 21st March in the presence of his son and a Jesuit priest, Father Origo, M le Blond. He slipped into unconsciousness and later in the day impoverished in his Venetian lodging house, the former Controller-General of French Finance died with great calmness and constancy.

> He departed this life on Monday last 21st of this month, giving us all his blessing; and he has made a general gift to your Ladys(hip) of all he had and all his pretensions whatsoever, with full power of disposing, acting contracting, etc. in short doing what you think proper of all; Knowing the kinde love you bear equally to us both, and other reasons which I'll acquaint yr Layds(hip) with when I shall wait on you at Paris.[27]

John Law's remains were settled in the church of San Gemigniano just one month short of his fifty-ninth year.

Hero or Hedonist?

Beelzebub begat Law,
Law begat the Mississippi
The Mississippi begat the Scheme,
The Scheme begat the Paper,
The Paper begat the Bank,
The Bank begat the Note,
The Note begat the Share,
The Share begat the Stockjobbing,
The Stockjobbing begat the Registration,
The Registration begat the Account,
The Account begat the general Balance,
The Balance begat Zero.
From which power of begetting was taken away.[1]

THERE ARE two broad schools of thought concerning John Law the man and John Law the economist and financier. One side presents him as a rather unattractive human being and broadly a negative influence on economic thinking and economic events. Those subscribing to this view tend to be writing in the eighteenth and early nineteenth centuries. The other side see him as a thinker born before his time and now understood as a financial genius. Though he may have indulged the delusion of personal grandeur at the expense of more rationale judgement when it was needed, in many ways he was an exceptional man who showed considerable fortitude when life's events turned against him. This perception is held by several modern biographers, economists, historians and investigative journalists.

The first school focuses on Law's human foibles and his personal self-indulgence. These perceived shortcomings are placed alongside a judgement that speaks of his investment and financial activities as deceitful, scheming, extravagant, prone to excess risk and steered essentially by megalomania. As might be expected, this overall negative perception of Law was upheld by those eighteenth-century French writers who ventured to comment upon the man and his business proceedings. For them, the general air that surrounded the collapse of the Royal Banque and the subsequent effects on French financial morale was too odious to pick out any sweetness or merits in Law's projects. This viewpoint held whatever stance they used to examine his work – Duclos and Saint-Simon, (journalism); Forbonnias (economics) and Montesquieu and Voltaire (politics).[2] Their decision is firm and unequivocal; John

Law was responsible for the great deal of human misery that resulted from the collapse of the System.

Until recently, French historians have also tended to present Law as indefensible. Pierre Heinrich writing in 1907 sees Law as a major influence on forced emigration to Louisiana.

These negative representations were also agreed by early English commentators. Horace Walpole described Law as a *very extraordinary man but not at all an estimable one.*[3]

The second school looks analytically at the misfortunate circumstances of Law's early London life and at the critical acumen displayed in his financial writings and his financial exploits.

Whatever the motives leading to his duel with Wilson, and whoever the main characters in intrigue with each man were, the truth behind the event did not surface then and it has not done since. The involvement of Elizabeth Villiers remains plausible, but over time the fight and its causes have become surrounded by satire and explanations bordering on the slanderous.

The duel did however shape the rest of Law's life. On the one hand, his flight led to positive opportunities to acquire in Europe first-hand observation of unfolding and novel banking systems, and unique financial ventures; on the other hand it set him in the roles of beau, gambler, escapist traveller and fugitive, and these characteristics have until more recent times veiled his economic prowess. This prowess may have been born of one lasting influence from the fiasco with Wilson, that of the insatiable desire to 'prove himself' of repute, honour and worth.

In highlighting Law's contribution to modern economic theory, the second school of opinion has acknowledged the key features of his enduring thinking. He is credited with seeing that credit can be a creative force for economic good. Paper money can represent the assets of a nation and the level of that representation can be manipulated to stimulate the production of commodities, and hence vibrant trade and innovative commerce. He also showed that difficult economic circumstances can be overcome by schemes other than those based on the burdens of increased taxation or reliance on extortionate loans.

In seeing that credit can temporarily outstrip current resources, he was in line with the modern system of maintaining national and international trade by using the fine balance between advance payment for development and investment, and audited collateral to shore up the venture – a forerunner then of the idea that projected capital can be represented in shares and these can run beyond the immediate assets held in money or stock. He transferred his gaming instinct by seeing that in reality most production, selling and buying, is a gamble of a kind. Commerce has to rest on people's willingness to invest in the hope of securing a greater return. Those investing have to hold faith in a positive outcome and to keep steady their belief in a stable and enduring world.

Today, we implicitly accept what Law preached. Our money has value to the extent of our faith in a viable tomorrow and not to the extent of the gold and silver we can obtain for it.[4]

He was adamant about the value of securing public and commercial confidence in a well-run national bank. He saw such a bank as the intermediary between the convenience of paper money and the security resting in the bank's vaults. His private bank based on his own funds and established in 1716 had issued 'notes' with an undertaking that reflected this security. *The Bank promises to pay the bearer at sight, the sum of…Crowns in coin of the weight and standard of this day, value received.*[5] This statement implied that notes would be honoured at the value established at the time of the exchange. However, by the time this bank had become the Royal Bank in December 1718, the promise had been watered down. *The Bank promises to pay the bearer at sight…livres in silver coin, value received.*[6] In effect, this meant the notes could be lowered in value on the whim of the Regent or his representative. Those with strong memories of recent reneging on debt and deposits by those of royal blood may well have taken this as an early sign that personal assets would not be so secure, now that the throne was once again associated with the money. Equally, they would know that controls on both banks lacked independent rigour. For example, Law's own bank had the Regent as patron and an inspector appointed by him.

The transfer to the Royal Bank brought no greater accountability.

> Years of broken promises and fiscal expediency had created a perfectly legitimate suspicion of the crown's fiscal operations. Without public accountability, hopes of transplanting English and Dutch banking practice to French soil were doomed to failure.[7]

In general, though he vacillated between respect for his fellows and frustration at their financial trembling and their tendency to be disobedient when compliance was needed, Law initially sought through his economic schemes the protection of their money and their assets. He thought this could be done best by well-governed trade and a secure central bank. He saw these as strong mechanisms to free people from exploitation by ruthless moneylenders and uncontrolled high interest rates. He also saw no reason why a national bank's assets should rest on gold alone. He believed the value of gold to be too much in the hands of those who controlled its supply.

More significantly, he held strongly to the view that a country's finances should be guided by rules and principles and that the tax burden should be universally distributed. He set down fourteen rules to establish this guidance and the sixth rule enunciates the idea that taxes should be imposed across the board and that the established abuses of the time – exemptions and privileges – worked against longer-term economic stability.

> Immunities, privileges and exemptions must be regarded as abuses which cannot be abolished soon enough. Clerics, noblemen or commoners, we are all equally subjects of the same king; it is against the nature of being a subject to aspire to be distinguished from others by the privilege of not paying tribute to his prince. What I say of the comparison between subjects I will also say of provinces, and of the comparisons between them; and in particular the clergy and nobility, being the two premier orders of the kingdom, should seek to distinguish themselves by their eagerness to contribute to the expenses of the State, rather than by immunities and exemptions. Nothing is more important for the good order of a kingdom than uniformity, and it is to be wished that it should reign in laws, customs and taxes.[8]

Though Law sincerely held this principle and believed in it wholeheartedly, he was not able to implement it during the time he held financial powers in France. He was debarred from doing so because the Regent had to preserve aristocratic interest to keep some state finance in place and to secure a platform of political stability.

Law's economic prowess has recently been put on a par with that possessed by Adam Smith and John Maynard Keynes. This may be true in respect of innovatory thinking to stimulate the trading process and the setting up of conditions to aid economic recovery.

Historical connection 13

It is possible that Law's contribution to the theory of money laid a foundation for later monetary theorists. He believed that money had no value outside the use made of it. He saw power in money only in so far that a good supply of it could create trade and through that activity generate a stock of treasure for the state.

> Domestick Trade depends on the Money. A greater Quantity employes more People than a lesser Quantity. A limited Sum can only set a number of People to Work proportion'd to it, and 'tis with little success Laws are made, for Employing the Poor or Idle in Countries where Money is Scarce.[9]

To Law, money was just one of many forms of commodity. He saw the abundance of money as a value only as a prerequisite to promote trade, labour, civic construction, population growth and general economic well-being. His suggestion to issue paper money in preference to coin was not an original proposal, though he perhaps made it more consistently than others at the time. What he emphasised was that when it was necessary to circulate money in abundance, paper was more suitable than metals.

He also believed its value needed to be underpinned by something that had greater stability than silver, hence his idea of 'land money'.

Adam Smith (1723-90) was also a Scot. He was born in Kirkcaldy and was initially educated at the local school. He went on to Glasgow University and Balliol College, Oxford. He went to live in Edinburgh in 1748 where he met the philosopher David Hume. Smith later undertook public lectures in Edinburgh and held two chairs at Glasgow University. By all accounts he was a very successful lecturer. His style was open debate rather than lectures based on dictated notes, and he engaged his audience in examining propositions by using Socratic discourse. This approach spread his reputation beyond student bodies and his propositions were discussed in various clubs and literary groups. Smith used a three-year Grand Tour of Europe to debate with leading thinkers in France the nature of a happy society and the means to ensure its wealth and stability. He followed his Grand Tour by living back in Kirkcaldy with his mother (Adam's father had died before he was born). During these quiet ten years, he published *Inquiry into the Nature and Causes of the Wealth of Nations.* Like John Law, he advocated the advantages of mutual trading and criticised the idea that the only form of wealth was gold. Also like Law, he suggested that any commodity was merely a token of need and a basis for exchange. He thought that the 'intercourse of trade' should not be thwarted because one country might choose to 'fasten down' the gold in the national treasure trove. In keeping with the philosophical mood of the time, Smith saw 'kind human nature' as the stability for trade – that men will choose a 'good and unselfish course' and therefore governments should not tie their hands with excessive legislation and by political attempts to control social affairs. Broadly then, Smith was a strong advocate of free trade and believed that economic good benefited from individual thrift and self-help. However, like Law, he saw social justice as the base feature of an enduring, settled and wealthy society.

> No society can surely be flourishing and happy, of which the far greater part of the members are poor and miserable. It is but equity, besides, that they who feed, cloath and lodge the whole body of the people, should have such a share of the produce of their own labour as to be themselves tolerably well fed, cloathed and lodged[10]

It is not certain to what extent Smith's economic thinking was influenced by Law's earlier work, but some suggest that Smith's *water/diamonds paradox* was taken *without acknowledgement* from Law.[11]

Adam Smith's own judgement on Law's commercial enterprise is neutral rather than condemnatory. Writing within his own time frame he described it as *the most extravagant project both of banking and stock-jobbing that perhaps the world ever saw.*[12]

John Maynard Keynes, Baron Keynes, (1883-1946) is primarily remembered as an economist.

He was, however, also a successful academic, philosopher, journalist, government adviser and company chairman. He was born in Cambridge and received much of his early education at home because of continuing bouts of sickness, though in later life he was noted for his commanding physical presence and his incisive intellectual rigour.

He went via Eton College to King's College, Cambridge. In August 1921, he published *A Treatise on Probability*, a work that had developed from a fellowship dissertation. The topic of probability had received some noteworthy attention from statisticians, but Keynes gave it a more significant philosophical slant. He believed that some rational weight could be attached to esoteric beliefs and opinions and these ideas would alter in their relationship to probability as the evidence available increased or changed. This work was to stand him in good stead later when in both theoretical and practical circumstances he was to consider economic fluctuations and the critical matter of the management of the economy.

He considered monetary theory in his two volumes, A *Treatise on Money*, published in 1930.

His rethinking on links between employment, money supply and interest rates appeared with the publication of his *General Theory of Employment, Interest and Money* in 1936.

In *A Treatise on Money*, Keynes briefly refers to John Law but he does not indicate whether the Scot's thinking was in any way an influence on his own. Some of Keynes's thinking certainly parallels John Law's. He did believe in managed currency in place of the 'gold standard' which he said was a 'barbarous relic'. He did not believe the economy was capable of self-adjusting over time, but believed in manipulation through financial agencies of control. Like Law, he thought that stimulating and sustaining trade required strategies to connect the money supply with the real economy. It is strange then that there is reference to Law but not his effect. Some are sure why this is so. *It may be surmised that Keynes avoids listing Law as one of his precursors because Law's System had failed.*[13]

Time and changes meant that Keynes was able to draw on more recent knowledge of world economic instability than Law. Price instability and instability in output and employment were significant throughout the lifetime of Keynes. He was in a position to experience first-hand and hence to consider in more depth the influences on world finance and world trade of national and international political decisions and political actions.

All three men used intuition to help them shape ideas as well as rational judgement. All three engaged in economic thinking to solve practical dilemmas and because they held a vision that good economic management helps all members of the community. All three were good communicators and they could work in the presence of vigorous opposition to their core ideas. All three believed in and gave a demonstration of the power of economic ideas to remedy some of the economic demands of the day. They were unequal to the task of controlling the economic waves of output, income, investment, inflation and unemployment, but then no following economic or political leader has fully succeeded with these difficult variables.

It is one thing to have prowess of any kind and another to apply it. Application calls for more than intellectual qualities. It rests as much on projection, flair, ingenuity and a willingness to take risks. Successful 'wheeler-dealers' often attract praise and honours. Those who fail are more likely to be held in contempt. Law did what many are now called to do; to find innovatory schemes and entrepreneurial solutions to keep the wheels of commerce turning. He put into practice many of the elements we now see in globalisation, worldwide marketing, international banking and interlinked stock market activity. In an age when 'mini-enterprise' is promoted as an essential part of the school curriculum, we must remember that Law was first and foremost an economic pioneer. For him the reward was exile but it could easily have been very different? What went wrong?

The influences John Law had to overcome were formidable. First, the French court and much of the French aristocracy had traditionally raised money on demand and often spent it recklessly. They did not fear accumulating debt and then reneging on it. Second, monetary and credit systems in Europe were few and far between, and the French systems were fragile. They were essentially in the hands of financiers who held significant hold over the economy and crown finance. They could literally charge what interest rates they liked because there was no attractive alternative like a secure national bank. Third, those persons with vested interest were determined to hold on to their power, even if it was bad for the country as a whole. They opposed Law's ideas mainly to protect their own self-interest. Fourth, Law had no existing system of credit to build on.

Law's calamitous schemes only confirmed what sensible men had known for centuries: the government could not be relied on to honour its debts. It was the resulting inability to borrow from the public which placed the state at the mercy of the financiers, allowing the latter to demand extortionate rates of interest. Lack of confidence in the government made the establishment of a central bank on the Dutch model impossible so money had to be raised through the personal credit of intermediaries.[14]

In giving Law the offices he had, the Regent had alienated bankers, nobles and other persons at Court. He faced consistent pressures to keep influential people on his side and to do so he tended to use company shares like confetti. This contributed to both the speculative frenzy and the rapidly arriving burst. The productive side of the economy could not keep pace with the over-production of bank notes and their rapid circulation. All too soon, many were left holding money not worth the notes bearing the amount.

Law's fundamental strength was his capacity to present clearly his economic vision and the theory on which it rested. He also saw that previous French financial administration emanated from vested interest and he sought to introduce a fairer system, ultimately with the type of accountability then becoming prevalent in the English and Dutch banking systems. In the early stages of his banking enterprise, he did succeed in carrying out many transactions such as discounting bills and money transfers at far lower interest rates than his competitors. This achievement drew from the Regent the comment: *I see why the bankers have risen in opposition to your establishment, they are not traders, they are thieves.*[15] An objective that Law had for the 'system' was to remove the French economy from its dependence on these 'thieves'.

In this area, however, Law did not move far from theory to successful policy. He failed to take out of the business market the main beneficiaries of earlier fiscal arrangements and he did not win the long power struggle to control the means of granting credit. *Once Law was exiled French financial administration continued as before.*[16]

Undoubtedly, John Law's own impulsive and ambitious nature contributed to the downfall. As time went on he was expected to be an 'enchanteur' (delightful magician) in respect of the 'system' and he tried to maintain this image. His rhetoric and actions extended across a vast range of developments. These included reimbursing the royal debt, consolidating the state bank, promoting investment in Louisiana, encouraging transfer of established means of wealth into suspended credit in the shares of an unproven Company, underpinning new taxation measures, developing trade opportunities in the East Indies and trying to open up other means of economic expansion and economic freedom. He was seen as a financial demi-god by all but the ardent sceptics. He was expected to get results over a vast range of investments and institutional changes and to get them very quickly. By and large he kept pace with expectations.

> So he had achieved, in less than four years, the ultimate monopoly: maritime and colonial trade, together with a bank of issue empowered to raise taxes, to coin and to print money. To maintain and exploit this mighty castle of credit he made regular issues of company shares: they were increasingly expensive but eagerly sought.[17]

With the early interest and early success, it was understandable that perhaps he came to believe he could ride all horses equally well and at the same pace. Later in his life, he acknowledged that this optimism left him disadvantaged.

> If I had the work to do over again I would proceed more slowly but more surely and I would not expose the country to the dangers which must necessarily accompany the sudden disturbance of generally accepted financial practice.[18]

Whether those needing quick results to repair the damaged French fiscal state, and those courtiers and citizens more motivated by sheer greed, would have let Law have the time for a more considered and leisurely approach is an open agenda. It is very unlikely and hence it is probably fair to say he was as much a victim of the haste as the instigator of it.

Certainly it is now recognised that Law did appreciate the four core values of money. Money is a measure of value, it is a medium of exchange, it stands as a system of credit, since it is a form of deferred payment, and it acts to represent a main 'store of wealth' held by individuals, companies and nations.

> Money is not a pledge, as some call it. It's a Value payed, or Contracted to be payed, with which 'tis supposed, the Receiver may, as his occasions require, Buy an equal Quantity of the same Goods he has Sold, or other Goods equal in Value to them: And that Money is the most secure Value, either to Receive, to Contract for, or to Value Goods by: which is least liable to a change in its value.[19]

He also understood that money is needed as a form of 'credit in advance' to increase notionally economic opportunities (for example, jobs) and economic output (saleable commodities). His basic idea is still very much in play today – money is made available to raise demand, which then transmits to raise production and supply, which in turn generates further money and further demand. John Law's fault was to be compliant with expanding the money supply too far too soon. He perhaps succumbed to the great pressure he was under to do so. The Regent was pressing such a line of action, those getting rich wanted more and those not yet on board were clamouring to be there. He was being praised for apparently handling and overcoming the French economic crisis, and the voices of those opposed to him, chiefly the financiers and others with vested interests, were somewhat muted by the apparent success of the system. Through these and other influences, he lost sight of the links between the overemphasised and false readings of the effects of money, against the real economy as it was operating in day-to-day terms. He also did not foresee the greedy hysteria that was to take over the minds of many French citizens.

In terms of economic theory, some see Law as belonging to the Mercantilist school. The bedrock of this school of thinking was the promotion of concrete links across the national economy, national trading and Merchant Capitalism. The key structure was an enduring bond between state interests and trading monopolies. Since at the height of the Mercantile System this bond extended across Europe and the New World, it was the vision and vigour that led to Amsterdam, Bruges, London and Venice becoming leading commercial cities. The bond was also behind the establishment of colonies in the Americas and the East Indies to protect national and company territorial interests.

Mercantilists regarded 'treasures' as the key marker of wealth. These might be newly established commodities such as tea and tobacco, but at centre stage were the hordes of new metals arriving from the New World, especially silver and gold. Commerce took on the guise of a trading war in respect of these key metals. The idea was to accumulate and keep as much silver and gold as was possible against those goods manufactured for sale to others. Equally, more treasure might be horded to underpin national wealth if goods currently imported were made at home.

In essence then, there was intense competition between nations to retain a high proportion of the key treasures as 'reserves' to pay for internal development and imperialist warfare. Powerful merchant monopolies appeared across Europe and these were manipulated to represent and sustain national interests. The underlying assumptions about national wealth became first *how important it is, both for peoples and for princes, that a kingdom should abound in gold and silver,*[20] and second that trade relied on import prohibitions and the creation of export surplus.

In subscribing to the view that a state must have a good stock of 'treasure' and see trade as a central consideration for economic well-being, Law shows mercantilist leanings. He differed of course from the conventional view of the time in believing that money as notes could replace metallic money and be used to transact credit and merchandising. In turn, these transactions would lead to an accumulation of valuable bullion in the state's treasury, thereby establishing and sustaining national wealth. In these respects he was a forerunner to how much of the modern world operates in commercial terms.

> But significantly the crash of 1720 had not destroyed the new circumstances which had produced it. By the mid-eighteenth century in western Europe, the worlds of trade, industry and public finance were more closely linked than they had ever been. All depended for their healthy functioning on a complex system of credit, and credit was grounded in the last analysis in the shifting sands of public confidence.[21]

The sheer scale of Law's overall personal and economic achievements is hard to envisage. Despite his murky and disreputable beginnings in connection with the duel and Beau Wilson's death, he emerged from debt and exile as an honourable man. His understanding of the laws of probability was most refined and on entry to France in 1714 he had amassed from his gambling a personal fortune. He went on to put an ambitious banking scheme into operation and to establish a trading company that was behind the colonisation of a large part of the United States. While developing both these ventures, he did much to extricate the French from their national debt and to point up fairer means of controlling state finances and taxation. Though not a native Frenchman by birth, he came to occupy one of the highest positions in French government, something akin to Robert Walpole's place as the first British Prime Minister. When his scheme and powers went into decline, he tried hard to reverse the loss and to limit the damage. He never lost faith in the underlying wisdom of developing an economy not reliant on gold and silver and in holding on to this belief he was a beacon on how things were to be.

At the human level, Law did not seek to protect his own wealth nor was he a man of mean personal disposition. He risked the significant wealth he brought to France to establish the *Banque Générale* and the *Compagnie des Indes*. When the collapse came he sought to contribute financially to aid some of those experiencing drastic loss. He is also said to have destroyed bills owing to him to keep some friends from feeling they had to honour them.

On the negative side, he did lose sight of his own maxim that 'confidence is nothing but the certainty of being paid' and he did underplay people's need to have something valuable that 'stores' that confidence.[22] He also supported an absolute regime that resorted to serious measures of constraint as the paper scheme began to collapse. The subsequent restriction on holding more than 500 livres in specie, the house searches to ensure no one was hoarding gold and the general measures to compel obedience to the state's authority seemed to be exonerated within Law's writing.

> I maintain that an absolute prince who knows how to govern can extend his credit further and find needed funds at a lower interest rate than a prince who has limited authority.[23]

Broadly speaking, he seems to have been somewhat 'schizophrenic' in his views and his actions concerning the avoidance of force and the use of force in seeking to stabilise public confidence. If he did believe fully in the power of despotic authority to stabilise financial crises, on this occasion the belief did not return a dividend for him. Panic quickly superseded state control, so that in the second part of 1720, the aroused public opinion and the desperate actions that followed rapidly laid his system to waste.

Perhaps more seriously, it is along the expansionary track of Law's economic venture where it is more difficult to rescue him from the charges of nepotism and the acquisition of personal wealth on the strained backs of others. The establishment of the Mississippi Company was a fresh impetus to French trade and investment. It held the potential to help the nation manage its financial crisis by providing a mechanism for paying creditors with shares for debts they were owed. By all accounts, tributaries from the Company continued to help the French economy long after Law's demise.

John Law's Company of the Indies, reconstituted and reorganised in the 1720s, played an important role in French commercial prosperity in the eighteenth century.[24]

In the early days, however, the Company was founded only on some embryonic commercial activities taking place in the very far away and sparsely populated Louisiana. Religious dissidents were not welcome and few migrants were willing to risk their lives on a perilous frontier. In truth, their stance was very sensible. Much of the Mississippi valley was still uncharted wilderness. A gap existed then between commercial aspiration and actual achievement and it had to be closed. It was closed by calculating and manipulative publicity.

The Company's propaganda machine issued flagrant appeals to investor greed: the mountains of Louisiana it seemed, were chockfull with gold, silver, copper, lead and quicksilver: fine wool almost leapt of the backs of the native sheep; the climate allowed not one but two annual harvests of rice and tobacco, and the natives were allegedly friendly (more than friendly in the case of the women, who were said to volunteer their sexual services joyfully to all comers).[25]

To expand rapidly the few hundred settlers in

Louisiana, it is claimed that between September and December 1719 Law used coercion to arrange forced marriages. Those forcibly married went out to Louisiana through La Rochelle.[22] Whether Law used such coercion or not, there were other forms of forced emigration to Louisiana and it is inconceivable that Law did not know about them. Despite protests from Governor Bienville that convicts, orphans, prostitutes and general undesirables were forming a substantial segment of the early population of the area, the need to convince investors that the colony was well founded and safely colonised ran over the governor's concerns about the type of people coming.

Bienville also had a second concern about populating the territory. He sent several requests to Paris for wives for the colonists, most especially for the Canadian soldiers billeted there. *Send me wives for my Canadians – they are running in the woods after Indian girls.*[26] The company responded before the *filles à la cassette* (1728) with groups of women sent from houses of correction, prostitutes from the street and teenage female orphans from Salpetiere and elsewhere. Despite their alleged reputation as 'women of ill repute' their arrival in the territory was a public spectacle.

When the ship carrying the females arrived at Ship Island near Biloxi earlier this year, women-hungry men paddled to the island in pirogues to greet them. Some of the women were married by a secular priest in Biloxi shortly after their arrival. The remaining women were parceled out to French settlements such as New Orleans, Mobile and Biloxi.[27]

An earlier biographer of Law is in no doubt that he was complicit in this human trafficking, if not directly then by default. He states that Law played a part in selling Louisiana as a 'new Eldorado' and did nothing to discourage public gullibility concerning that territory and the potential consequences of investment there.[28]

It is also clear that John Law had a hand in the slave trade, if not directly, then through his quest to expand the population of Louisiana by all means possible. The city of Nantes developed a thriving port by shipping 'ebony' (Africans) to the new land. This involvement can only discredit Law in modern eyes. He connived with what has been described as *all the wealth piled by the bond-man's 250 years of unrequited toil*.[29] Yet many who ostensibly denounced slavery, invested in it at the time (Voltaire).[30] Equally, many men of later eminence held, worked and punished slaves (Washington).[31] Perhaps on this matter, Law's actions can only be fairly judged in the context of the time.

So is John Law best described as a hero or a hedonist? A balanced jury might conclude he showed signs of being both. As a man he demonstrated several of the characteristics apparent in popular descriptions of heroism. At the height of his fame he was, at one and the same time, of striking presence, a reputed 'beau', a successful gambler, adventurer, traveller, banker, royal courtier of rank and international businessman. He was strong and in large measure honourable when facing the fortitudes that life handed out to him. The tragic affair with Wilson does not seem to be a case of malice aforethought and he did not surrender to anyone the names of those who assisted him at this very low point in his life. He bore both prison and exile with a fair measure of stoicism. He seems to have worked his way through debauchery to a stable relationship with Katherine and throughout his more troubled latter years he was as loyal as circumstances permitted to his mother, wife, brother and children.

He remained resolute in promoting and defending his monetary systems and time has shown these to be based on some intellectual and practical rigour. They also seem to be based on an overarching economic plan as opposed to a set of piecemeal 'on the hoof' actions and features. His ideas cohered over time into a grand vision – *a sequence of ideas which are interlinked and which reveal more and more the principle on which they are based.*[32]

He remained largely focused on his duty when thrust into being the person at the centre of the most manic period of stock-exchange the world has ever known. He worked intensely to recover the situation against formidable odds, and only left France when required to do so. He accepted impoverished circumstances without much complaint, and tried frankly and honestly to make others accept that these circumstances were his true final lot.

There were periods in his life when he seemed to believe the doctrine that true value lies only in the pursuit of pleasure in general and sensual indulgence in particular. There were also times when he was somewhat megalomaniacal in his dealings with others. However, his hedonism in these guises appears to be of mild order compared to other grandees of the day, and other notables born long after him.

In his general approach to political and social matters, he sought collaboration not conflagration, and in his transactions overall he sought to unite, not divide. His personal disposition towards potential seeds of national disruption is reflected in his early writing:

> Altho' heaven and earth calls upon us at this time, to defend and vindicate our rights and libertys in particular, and to take effectual care, that this kingdom may be under other and more tolerable circumftances, with our neighbour nation in the next age, than it hath been in this, yet the meafures to be taken even with relation to them ought not to be inflaming, but healing; fince we embarked in one common caufe, the defence of religion and liberty, where every good subject ought to play his part, let therefore our deportment in this manner be fuch as may be capable of

convincing, that we are not only in the right point of fact; but likewise in point of good conduct and management.[33]

His personal motto was 'neither obscure nor low'. This sentiment fits his economic portrait very well. His writings on economic schemes and fiscal matters are generally lucid and exemplified. His thinking is expansive and he sketched out a macroeconomic approach to banking, credit and money management. The broad sweep of what he described in 1705 is not dissimilar to the systems in operation today. He recognised that the circulation of money supply can create productivity, cyclical trade and full employment. He considered public credit to be a powerful control on economic activity. He envisaged an international monetary system that was not tied to precious metals such as gold and silver. He knew that much of daily economic life is a pendulum swinging between private and public interests, between intuitive confidence and hopeful aspiration, and between subjective and objective evidence about performance.

Such was the issue of Law's celebrated system, which left the world a lesson which the world was slow to learn, that the enlargement of the circulation quickens industry so long only as the enlargement continues, for prices then rise, and every king of labor is remunerated; that, when this increase springs from artificial causes it must meet with a check, and be followed by a reaction; that, when the reaction begins, the high remunerating prices decline, labor fails to find an equivalent, and each evil opposite to the previous advantage ensues; that, the reform, every artificial expansion of the currency, every expansion resting on credit alone, is a source of confusion and ultimate loss to the community, and brings benefits to none but those who are skilled in foreseeing and profiting by the fluctuations.[34]

After the collapse of the 'system' Law was seen as a villain who symbolised regal power and state deception at its worst. Given that he did not play the pivotal role in shaping the collapse, he never accepted any wrongdoing of the villainous kind. He certainly did not mastermind a massive fraud and he did not make grotesque misleading statements of the kind seen from international companies in recent times. His fatal flaw was his desire to see economic activities as he wished them to be, not as they were. His major error was his failure to judge the characters closest to him and the agenda they were pursuing at his expense. He paid heavily for this failure. He had to spend the rest of his days with his reputation in shreds, his economic knowledge chased for ulterior motives and with the ever-present risk of further incarceration.

The jury is still out deciding just what interrelated

political, social and economic factors made John Law's system fail, but few now doubt he was basically an honest man and an economic planner who bordered on the genius. The intellectual rigour brought to his arguments place him well beyond the roles of just speculator and adventurer. He is rightly regarded as a significant monetary theorist and one who earned his status by being an original thinker and self-made economist. Despite the tragic end to his visionary system and his life, he ought to have a justified and assured place in any hall of fame for those who have made a significant contribution to the theory and practice of economics.

> Having regard to the circumstances of the time, to the rudimentary conditions of monetary science; and to the want of national experience in credit transactions, he displayed both wonderful originality and wonderful soundness. But in spite of the catastrophe (the fall of the System) John Law may have been an excellent financier; just as Napoleon was a great soldier in spite of Waterloo.[35]

The John Law Trail

Lauriston Castle

The castle is near Cramond. It lies in attractive grounds beside the Firth of Forth. It is not so much a castle in the traditional sense, as a villa derived from an earlier tower house. It is just three miles from the centre of Edinburgh, and the grounds and views are spectacular. William Law acquired the property in 1683 but none of the Law family lived there. John owned the house until he sold it back to his mother in 1693 to help settle his debts. The house has a long and distinguished history. Fortunately, the last owner, Mrs Reid, *left the castle, content and grounds to the Nation in 1926.*[1] It remains much as she left it – including a warm and impressive Edwardian interior.

Paris – arrondissement 3 – rue Quincampoix

This very narrow passageway has been in existence since around 1200. The name changes across the centuries from Quiquempoit to Cinquampoit to Quincampoix. Today it is about 450 metres in length.

At the lower end it connects with the rue des Lombards and it terminates at rue Aux Ours. The rue Aubrey Le Boucher and the rue Rambuteau act as crossways that divide the Quincampoix into three distinct sections. All three sections constitute little more than narrow alleyways providing road width of only around three to eight metres. In walking the full length of the rue, one can see why, when it was the centre of speculative dealings in Mississippi shares, all forms of transport were excluded. Equally, though during the Mississippi boom the street was gated at both ends, with one access for nobles and the wealthy, and another for the general public, once inside the narrow confines of the street, all rank was lost – '…*lost in the motley crowd of speculators shouting, gesticulating, waving papers and counting money.*'[2] The prevailing turmoil that surrounded all the dealing ensured that nobility rubbed shoulders with artisans, priests with members of the laity, doctors with patients and honest dealers with unscrupulous sharks.

Between the summer of 1719 and the summer of 1720, the street was home to some of the wildest speculation seen in the history of trade, Before the crash, Mississippi shares change hands at rapidly escalating

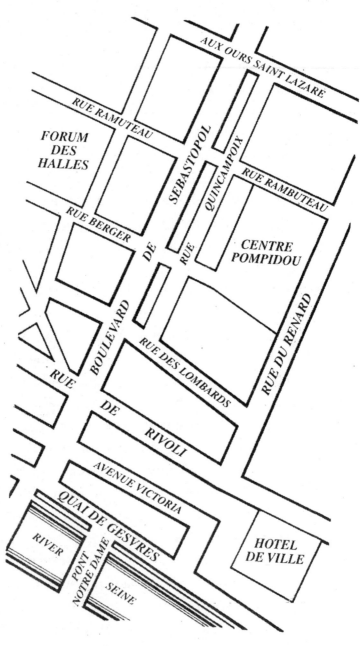

12   The location of the rue Quincampoix.

prices. The narrowness of the street and the regular habiting crowds meant there was little easy communication down its length, hence it was said that prices at one end of the alley were often very different from the other.

> The public were enthusiastic about the stock. In Paris, people of every class enjoyed the novelty of making a fortune while they slept. Rags became riches, and riches became inordinate riches. So many people were becoming rich that the French needed a new word to describe them, and 'millionaire' was it.[3]

As the speculation became excitable commotion rather than reasoned communication, fortunes were made and lost within the hour. Outrageous rents were levied and paid for rooms in the street and those of quick wit created opportunities to make wealth on the fringes of the trading. For example, anecdote holds that in aiding the speculation *a cobbler earned 200 livres a day supplying pens and paper...and his booth, a hunchback netted 150,000 livres for the use of his hump* as a desk, and a soldier who used his *unusually broad shoulders...similarly...made sufficient to obtain his discharge.* Large sums of money were also made by *caterers,* and, as many speculators arrived from outside Paris, enhanced prices were paid for *coach tickets.*[4] Servants or agents sent to the rue to sell shares cunningly *would wait until the shares had risen so many points, and then conclude their purchase and pocket the difference…a valet is said to have made fifty million…*and for a time the street contributed to some social rebalance: a cook dressed expensively and taking a box at the opera next to the mistress exclaimed, *'I have become rich and I dress up out of my wealth. I owe nothing to anyone. I like dressing up, so I dress up. That hurts no one. What objection can you have to that?'*[5]

Many people across all social ranks and the professions became obsessed with the day-to-day state of Mississippi stock. As with trading today, information and rumour leaked from the Quincampoix caused celebration, consternation or confusion. The Regent's physician Chirac learned on his way to a patient that prices were sliding. It is said that *while taking the lady's pulse he cried, 'My God, it falls! It falls!'*[6] He was required immediately to repair his reputation and reassure his patient that her death was not imminent.

Inevitably, in such mayhem of anxiety, unregulated trading and unconventional social intercourse, mob behaviour and violence did not stay away. The market quickly became bullish and there were many instances of robbery, aggressive behaviour and general lawlessness. Even the Regent's mother became concerned by it all: *'…not a single night passes but one finds people murdered for the sake of banknotes.'*[7]

All this disturbance in a street that was far from clean and where evasion or escape were near impossible.

The inconvenience of the darkest and nastiest street in Paris does not prevent the crowds of people of all qualities…coming to buy and sell their stocks in the open place; where, without distinction, they go up to their ankles in dirt, every step they take.[8]

As it became clear that the expansion was unsustainable and as Law's enemies started again to use the hand of doubt over his intent and his capacity to make the system stable, rue Quincampoix and the surrounding streets became home to yet more gross disorder, violence and murder. An historical plaque sited where the street joins the rue des Lombards records one of the most memorable of the crimes committed.

Historical connection 15

The rue de Venise connects with the rue Quincampoix. At this intersection the cabaret L' Epée-de-Bois opened in 1658. It became the home of dance and violin masters, and by 1719 it was a well-known tavern famed for its musical events. At this time it also attracted many wealthy customers because it was favourably situated for access to number 65 in the rue Quincampoix – the office of the *Banque Générale de Law*.

On 22nd March 1720, Count Antoine Joseph de Horn (also known as young Comte de Horn) arrived at the tavern with two accomplices. They came to meet a stockholder called Lacroix on the pretext of buying shares from him. Their real motive was robbery to help pay off gambling debts. They targeted Lacroix because they were reliably informed that he usually had on his person large sums of money.

In a back room they threw a tablecloth over the broker's head and stabbed him ferociously. His cries were heard and a quick-thinking tavern employee locked the room. All three jumped through the window, resulting in a sprained ankle for de Horn. This led to a vain attempt by him to claim he was one of the victims. The quick arrest of the other two, however, soon confirmed his involvement.

Horn was sentenced to be 'broken on the wheel' – a barbaric form of execution. The prisoner was tied to the side of a cylindrical wheel so that they were fully stretched across the spokes. One or more executioners would then use heavy iron bars to break first arms, then legs, then thighs and finally the 'blow of mercy' to the chest. The last blow was so called because it normally finished the poor recipient and relieved them from further agony. Occasionally their relief came in the form of a garrotte. For more barbarous effects, the wheel could be suspended and turned over a trench of fire. It is said that the death of Saint Catherine of Alexandria 'on the wheel in this way' is now immortalised in the 'Catherine wheel' firework.

In France, death on the wheel was usually reserved for spies and common criminals. As de Horn had some regal links, the Regent was petitioned to show either mercy or to arrange death by the more rapid and usual form of execution, beheading by sword or axe. However, the Regent regarded the crime as particularly atrocious. He responded with his now infamous quote *La crime fait la honte, et non pas l'échafoud.*[9] (It is the crime that is the shame, not the scaffold.) For his part Horn seems to have become reconciled to his fate. *I deserve the wheel; I had hoped that out of consideration for my family, the penalty would be changed to decapitation; I am resigned to all so as to obtain the pardon of my crime from God.* He did though enquire of the prison chaplain, '*Do people suffer much on the wheel?*'[10]

Watched by a large, raucous crowd, de Horn underwent the gruesome execution in the Place de Greve on 26th March 1720. He was just twenty-two years old. He took nearly an hour to die.

It was said that *Mr Law convinced the Regent of the absolute necessity of making a severe example of that criminal at a time when many carried their whole fortune in their pockets.*[11]

It is more likely that the Regent took solace in the popular support his decision attracted. He told his mother that the people say *whenever someone does something against the Regent personally, he forgives everything and does not punish him; but when something is done against us, he takes it very seriously and does it justice, as you can see by this comte de Horn.*[12]

Philippe d'Orléans also extended the idea of being 'broken on the wheel' to describe the fate he felt those debauchees he spent his leisure time with deserved. His link of the French term 'roué' (literally wheel) with this idea became associated through extension to how 'roué' is sometimes used now. It has taken on the meaning of debauched or lecherous rake.[13]

Execution on the wheel probably ended in France with the Revolution. Then Dr Joseph Ignace Guillotin proposed that criminals should be speedily beheaded on the grounds of 'égalité'. The Constituent Assembly passed the necessary degree and the initial guillotine was constructed by a German engineer. It was first used on 25th April 1792.

The L'Epée de Bois became the basis for the Royal Academy of Music and the famous Paris Opera.

In walking through the rue Quincampoix today, one sees contemporary art galleries, body adornment shops, an international coffee emporium and the Théâtre Molière Maison De La Poesie – the latter being a reminder that many streets in Paris had little theatres before Napoleon closed most of them in 1807. What is difficult to envisage as you now traverse the street are the throngs of speculators, merchants, entertainers and bankers who made or lost fortunes here when the 'system' was all. It is even more difficult to envisage that the street was the centre of the frenzy that attracted Voltaire's swinging cynicism.

> It is good to come to a country when Plutus is turning all heads in the city. Have you really all gone mad in Paris? I only hear talk of millions. They say that everyone who was comfortably off is now in misery and everyone who was poverty-stricken bathes in opulence. Is this a reality? Is it a chimera? Has half the nation

13 The narrow rue
Quincampoix as it is
today.

found the philosopher's stone in the paper mills? Is Law a god, a rogue, or a charlatan who is poisoning himself with the drug he is distributing to everyone?[14]

Paris – arrondissement 5 – Scots College, rue du Cardinal Lemoine

The college developed from a religious foundation established on a farm at Grisy-Suines in 1325. The intention was to allow ecclesiastical and secular students from Moray in Scotland to study within proximity to the University of Paris. Most, but not all of the students were from Catholic families. Many, but not all of them became priests. They were expected to be Scots either by birth or by close descent, although there were exceptions. Those not Scot by birth gained entry by financial influence or through patronage.

There were periods of tension between Scots College in Paris and Scots College in Rome. At various times, the latter college tried to poach students and to seek influence on those who should gain entry to the register in Paris. Scots College Paris became more strongly associated with the Jacobite cause, than did its counterpart in Rome.

The Paris college commenced at rue des Fosses–Saint-Victor (now rue Cardinal Lemoine) in 1665. The chapel was added in 1672. The college existed for around 190 years. The attractive original façade survives. Near the front door is a heritage sign. The premises now house an *École Privée* (Saint Genevieve).

John Law recognised his father's resting place by donating to the college fifty shares in the East India Company.

14   Scots College, Paris.

Each share was then quoted at 9.000 livres tournois, making a total of 450,000 livres, a very large sum in that day. Ill-fatedly, however, after the fall of Law's system, the French government nullified the bequest, and although Chevalier Andrew Michael Ramsay managed to get the actions restored to the college, the shares had dropped to one-fourteenth of their original value.[15]

In 1752, John's brother William Law was also laid to rest in the chapel college. Though not always stalwart in supporting Katherine in the years of his brother's exile, he eventually did seek to have his own children benefit from debts owed to John. The attempt dragged on for

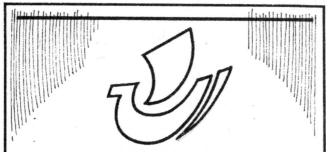

Histoire de Paris
Collège des Ecossais

L'immeuble sur rue a été construit de 1662 a 1665 par Robert Barclay qui dirige le collège et le séminaire des Ecossais. Achevée èn 1672, la chapelle possède un mausolée ou repose dans une urne en bronze doré le cerveau de Jacque il d'Angleterre, mort à Saint-Germain en Laye en 1701. Transformé en prison sous la Terreur, le collège fut rendu à l'eglise anglais en 1806, et loué par un el ablissement d'ensegnement

15   The historical significance of Scots College.

decades and a settlement in their favour was not agreed until 1779. By this time a sum estimated at around four million livres had been reduced to *the piddling sum of 37,545 francs and four sous.*[16] It was William's grandson, Jacques Alexandre Bernard, who as military governor of Venice was able to move Law's remains from the Church of Gemigniano in 1808.

Louisiana

John Law never did visit the territory. He was too busy with the 'system' first at its height and then struggling to rescue it from collapse. The downside of this pressure was twofold. Law had no real understanding of the territory and its potential, so its initial development by the Company was largely opportunistic. Also, to quote today's business language, there was no overall strategic plan, and so progress was essentially irregular.

After the loss of the bank in November 1720, the Mississippi Company floundered. Various strategies were used to try to stabilise the situation and to aid recovery. Most were questionable morally.

In the immediate period after Law's departure from Paris, many of the 6,000 or so people then in Louisiana faced hunger and hardship. This was almost inevitable. The colony was dependent on France and the French economy for trade and supplies. Many people chose to try their luck elsewhere in North America and several of those remaining in the territory stayed poor and disadvantaged. The population rapidly declined and in 1752 the Company gave over its concessions, and the territory became a crown colony. In the years that followed, French interests in Louisiana were to be further disadvantaged during and after the Seven Years' War.

Historical connection 16

The Seven Years' War arose from the contrary colonial ambitions of England and France. Some historians regard the conflict as the true First World War. It was wide-scale and embraced three continents. In mainland Europe – Russia, Austria and France tried to encircle Prussia and in India and in North America there was Anglo-French conflict.

The capture of Quebec and Montreal in Canada removed French power in that country and the dominance of British Sea power ensured that other territories in America could not be sustained or retained by France.

In a peace treaty signed at Fontainebleau in November 1762, France ceded Upper Louisiana to Spain. Officially France gave over the area as compensation for Spain's territorial losses during the

Seven Years' War. By this time, however, France was also finding it difficult to maintain any hold in North America. They had met with defeat in Canada and they could no longer defend territory west of the Mississippi. As part of the peace negotiation, Britain acquired the French possessions east of the Mississippi.

The transfer to Spanish control did not please the local populace. It was two years before they were told the transfer had taken place and there was no significant Spanish presence in the territory until 1766. By then, disquiet with the enforced arrangement was running high. The new governor, Antonio de Ulloa, met such resistance he fled to Cuba. The peoples of Louisiana continued to revolt against the Spanish and, by so doing, they became the first colonists in the New World to take a stand against subservience to European power.

On August 18, 1769, however, Don Alejandro O'Reilly, accompanied by 2056 soldiers, succeeded in imposing Spanish authority.[17]

Spain agreed to give Louisiana back to France in 1800. At that time:

Less than one per cent of the area was settled. The creoles, numbering with their slaves about 40,000 in 1800, were concentrated on both banks of the lower Mississippi. There was a few garrisons and trading posts on the west bank of the river between New Orleans and St Louis, and a few more on the Red river; the rest was in possession of the Indians. Sugar cane and cotton had recently been introduced from the West Indies.[18]

The Spanish and French agreement troubled the newly inaugurated Thomas Jefferson who thought that a resurgent France under Napoleon might restrict access to the mouth of the Mississippi. He wrote – *There is on the globe one single spot, the possessor of which is our natural and habitual enemy. It is New Orleans.*[19] He instructed Robert B Livingston, minister in France, to press that American rights to New Orleans be honoured. He also established negotiation to purchase West Florida in case that area was to be subject to new French possession. In so doing, he showed significant insight. Napoleon sent an army to reclaim Saint Dominique from the island slaves who had taken control in 1801, but the French were not successful due to continuing Haitian resistance and the ravages of yellow fever. Not able to foresee this eventuality, Jefferson prepared to act with the despised recent adversary Britain, to stop the French taking over again in New Orleans.

Tension rose in 1802 when Spain, still in possession of Louisiana, revoked all rights to use New Orleans and Jefferson, thinking incorrectly the French hand was behind the restriction, sent James Monroe to offer ten million for New Orleans and Florida. By this time Napoleon was preparing a new offensive in Europe and did not want to spare troops to the task of holding New World interests. He was also in need of money for his new campaigns. Early in 1803, before Monroe reached Paris, Napoleon, through his Foreign Minister Talleyrand, had agreed to sell all of Louisiana west of the Mississippi to the United States for $15 million. This was about four cents an acre.

The territory gained population from Law's Mississippi Scheme. The French established the first permanent settlement around 1714, Law's monopoly on commerce brought other French people, including the *filles à la cassette,* and by 1720 there were also German farmers from the Upper Rhine. From 1755 forward, the British expelled French settlers from Acadia in Nova Scotia. These Acadians went to Louisiana and became the Cajuns.

Louisiana became the eighteenth state on 18th April 1812. Additional territory was added in 1819 to form the current state boundaries.

Marble Hill, Twickenham, Greater London

Built for Henrietta Howard, a friend to Law in his hour of need, the house was completed in 1729 the year of his death. The design arose from collaboration between Roger Morris and Lord Herbert. By the time she came to occupy it, Henrietta was more or less detached from court life. She became countess of Suffolk in 1731 and the house reflects something of her capabilities and her later character and interests. She established a large circle of friends and her visitors included Alexander Pope and Horace Walpole. Her later years were a struggle with debt but when she died at Marble Hill on 26th July 1767 she was able to pass the house to her nephew Lord Buckinghamshire. The house eventually came into the care of English Heritage in 1986.

Chiesa Di San Moisé, Venezia (Church of San Moisé, Venice)

The origins of the church date to the ninth century. It was however rebuilt in the sixteenth century after an earthquake. It is dedicated to the prophet Moses.

There is one central aisle leading to the high altar and two adjoining chapels. There are numerous paintings, frescoes and monuments. The paintings include Bambini's *Moses and the Eternal Father in Glory* (ceiling), Pellegrini's *The Calamity of the Snakes* (left of the high altar) and Brusaferro's *The Crossing of the Red Sea* (right of the high altar). The visitors' notes in English (2004) conclude with the statement:

> A CURIOSITY: before going out, on the floor of the Church, near the central door, there is a tombstone, coming from the Church of San Gemigniano, of Giovanni Law, French banker and adventurer, buried in Venice.[20]

John Law instructed Pellegrini to complete paintings and interior decorations for the rooms of the Banque Royale in Paris (Sani 1996). Pellegrini was the brother-in-law of the Venetian artist Rosalba Carriera. On return to her native city, at a time when she is said to have known that John Law was there, some say she proclaimed with vigour that Law never paid Pellegrini for the work. Others say the artist was not disposed this way and she stayed loyal to the Law family.[21] What is clear is that in a more harmonious time, Rosalba herself had completed a crayon portrait of Law. After his death this went with the young John to Paris but subsequently came into the possession of Horace Walpole. He sold it on in 1824 and it is not known if it still exists. Rosalba continued her work and became an established pastellist and portrait painter. Some of her work was acquired by George III for the royal collection. Over 100 items were held in the Rosalba Room in a gallery at Dresden belonging to Frederick-Augustus (later Augustus III of Poland) but these were passed on or destroyed during World War II.

The grand ceiling illustrated by Pellegrini was to share the fate of Law's system. It collapsed towards the end of 1728. John Law took this as an omen. *'The material witnesses of my work have been destroyed. I have a strong feeling that my own existence is about to disintegrate with them.'*[22]

16   The Church of San Moisé.

The principal milestones in John Law's life

1671	Born in Edinburgh. Baptised on 21st April.
1683	His father, William Law, dies in Paris.
1691	John moves to London.
1692	Sells his rights of inheritance to Lauriston to his mother.
1694	Kills Edward Wilson in a duel (9th April). Condemned to death but escapes to the Continent.
1694– 1705	Visits, works and gambles in several European countries. Studies more formally the

principles of banking and finance. Becomes attracted to Bank of Amsterdam and newly established Bank of England.

1703-04   Writes the *Essay on a Land Bank*.

1705   Returns to Scotland. Writes *Money and Trade Considered*.
          Proposals to Edinburgh Parliament for a trading corporation and the stimulating use of paper money. Proposals rejected.

1707   Union of Scotland and England. Returns to the Continent and settles in France. Later expelled from France for excessive gambling. Gains more knowledge of banking and credit systems.

1712   Louis XIV grants Antoine Crozat exclusive rights to trade in Louisiana.

1713   Law returns to Paris. By now he has in-depth knowledge of the banking and credit systems operating in other parts of Europe.

1715   King Louis XIV dies. Philippe d'Orléans becomes Regent of France. Law proposes foundation of French bank. Proposal is rejected.

1716 Status of Frenchman acquired through naturalisation. Establishes a note-issuing bank, Law & Co or the General Bank.
Banque Générale becomes the *Banque Royale* (December). Extends monopoly across most of French overseas trade. Company name changed to Compagnie des Indes.

1717 Crozat sells his Louisiana rights to John Law. Law creates Compagnie d'Occident or Mississippi Company. Takes over monopoly of Louisiana trade. Government annuities accepted to purchase shares.

1719 Pardoned by George I for killing Edward (Beau) Wilson – but this is yet to be ratified in an English Court.

1720 Becomes *Contrôleur général* of French finances. Converts to Catholicism. Later in the year has to leave France with little money and few possessions. Arrives in Brussels in late December. Moves on to Venice at the beginning of the New Year.

1721 Travels to Copenhagen. Returns from there to London courtesy of Sir John Norris, admiral of Baltic squadron. On 28th of November, pleads at the bar of the King's

Bench his majesty's pardon for the murder of Edward Wilson.

1723   Philippe d'Orléans, Regent of France dies on the 2nd December. Law's hope of reviving his financial status in France is extinguished. He loses his pension.

1725   Leaves London for the last time. Travels with his son John and a nephew to Aachen, ostensibly to work in the interest of British foreign policy. In this capacity, moves on in 1726 to Munich.

1726   Requests and is given permission to retire from his 'overseas duties'. Returns to Venice.

1727   Finishes writing the history of his official duties in France. Meets the Stuart Pretender.

1728   Shares his experiences in France with Montesquieu. Debates with him the merits of his 'system'.

1729   Dies in Venice (21st May) aged fifty-eight. His remains interred in the church of San Gemigniano in the Piazza San Marco.

1808   Great nephew, Jacques Alexandre Bernard

Law, uses his status as military governor of Venice to re-inter Law's remains in the nearby Church of San Moisé.

Notes

(The sources bearing only author and date are listed in full in the bibliography.)

Introduction

1   Ferdinando Galiani, quoted by Fraser Hosford in *John Law, Monetarist or Keynesian*, p.1 – Internet version.

2   Common description of Law circulating in Paris circa 1720-1730. Quoted in various texts concerning his life and work.

3   Geoffrey Treasure 1985, *The Making of Modern Europe: 1648-1780*, p.302, Methuen, London, 1985.

4   Alfred Marshall, *Money Credit and Commerce*, p.41, London 1924.

5   Karl Marx, Capital, iii p.573, London 1981.

6   Davidson, 1971.

7   John Kenneth Galbraith, quoted in *The Oxford Companion to British History*, 1997, p.565.
8   Wood, p.149.
9   Schumpter, J A (1954), *History of Economic Analysis*, p.295, Oxford University Press, London.
10 Horne 2002, p.166.
11 Source unknown.
12 Charles Dickens Jnr, 1875.
13 In Gerhold, 1999.

Conception to Crime

1   Wood, 1824, p.1.
2   Hyde, 1969, p.20 (quoting George Lockart, Jacobite politician and author).
3   Wood, 1824, p.164.
4   Wood, 1824, p.6.
5   Jager, 2005, preface.
6   Holmes, 2001, pp.284-288.
7   Hutton, 1992.
8   Pugin (1762-1832) in St Aubyn 1985, p.92.
9   Glendinning, 1998, p.129.
10 Murphy, 1997, pp.24-34.
11 Gleeson, 1999, pp.59-60.
12 Glendinning, 1998, p.47.

1   Hyde, 1969, p.35.

2   Woods, 1824.

3   Haley, 1972.

4   Law, 1705. (p.14 Internet version. Also quoted in Montgomery Hyde, pp 38-39.)

5   Illustration in the Money Gallery – British Museum.

6   *Lettres Patentes du Roy Portent Privilege en favour du Sieur Law et sa Compagnie d'etablir une Banque Generale. (Article III).*

7   John Keyworth, *Forgery The Artful Crime: A Brief History Of The Forgery Of Bank Of England Notes*, Bank of England Museum Publication, 2001.

8   Davies, 2002.

9   The Mercenary Souldier, 1646.

10 Law, *Essay on a Land Bank,* also quoted in Murphy 1997, p.58.

11 Law, *Essay on a Land Bank,* also quoted in Murphy.

12 Valdez, 1998.

13 Betts, p.7.

14 Southgate, 1949, p.78.

15 Quoted in Horne, 2002, p.163.

16 McFarland Davis, 1887, p.3.

17 Doyle, 1978.

18 Horne, 2002, p.164.

19 Colin James, 2002, p.60.

20 Campbell quoted in Upton, 2001, p.248.

21 Murphy, 1997, p.4.

22 Lande 1982, pp.10-11.

23 McFarland Davis, 1887, pp.10-11.

24 Lande, 1982, p.6.

25 Clifton, 1995 p.93.

26 Davidson, p.103.

27 Clifton, 1995 p.93.

Finance to Flight

1 Betts, p.7.

2 *Letters of Madame Charlotte Elizabeth de Basiere, Duchess of Orleans*, vol ii, p.274.

3 Rude p. 203.

4 Treasure, 1985, p.304.

5 Horne, 2002, pp.165-166.

6 Stewart, quoted in Woods, p.119.

7 Saint Simon.

8 Schama, 2001.

9 O'Gorman, 1997, p.70.

10 Upton, 2001, p.248.

Debacle to Death

1 A lampoon describing the 'system'. Quoted in various sources (e.g. Hyde, p.158).

2 Pevitt 1997, p. 269.

3 ibid, p.73.

4 Hyde, 1969, p.169.

5   Versari, Professor Artemio, Notes accompanying the collection *Musical instruments – The Baroque in Venice*, Museo della Musica, Venice, 2004.

6   Pierre Crozat – in a letter to the Venetian Artist Rosalba Carriera.

7   De Bono.

8   Wood, 1824, p.3.

9   Earl of Stair – quoted in Montgomery, 1969.

10 John Law to Count Von Sinzendorf, Austrian Minister.

11 Wood, p.169.

12 Gleeson, 1999, p.65.

13 Black, 2001, pp.3-4.

14 Hyde, 1969, pp.185-86.

15 Wood, p.170.

16 Hervey, 1931.

17 Baird, 2003, p.50.

18 Hyde, p.171 – see also Wood, p.174.

19 Quoted in most sources on Law – for example, Hyde, 1969, p.194.

20 Deuteronomy 1:22 NIV.

21 William Congreve (1670-1729) in *The Double Dealer.*

22 Quoted in most sources on Law – e.g. see Hyde 1969, pp.205-06.

23 Stewart, 2002.

24 Hyde, 1969, p.207.

25 John Law speaking to the visiting French Consul. (Hyde, p. 208.)

26   Colonel Bruges – letter to Whitehall – Hyde, p.208 and Murphy, p.324.

27   Letter from John Law's son to his mother. (Quoted on most sources on Law – e.g. Murphy, p. 326.)

Hero or Hedonist?

1   Placard said to be posted all over Paris after the fall. Lande / Erlich, p.10.

2   Minton, 1975, p.266.

3   Professor Paul Harsin, 'Le Banque et le Systeme de Law', in J G Van Dillen's *History of the Principal Public Banks,* The Hague 1934.

4   Minton, 1975, p.266.

5   Wood, 1824, pp.29-32.

6   Wood 1824, pp 29-32.

7   Julian Swann, p.200 in William Doyle (Ed), *Old Regime France 1648-1788,* Oxford University Press 2001.

8   Quoted in *John Law, oeuvres completes*, vol 3, pp 39-61, ed P Harsin, 1934.

9   John Law, *Money and Trade Considered,* 1705, Internet version, p.4.

10   Smith quoted in *Oxford Dictionary of National Biography,* Vol. 51, 2004, p.22.

11   Minton, 1975.

12   Adam Smith, *An Enquiry in the Wealth of Nations, Book II,* p.283, 1776.

13   Quoted in Murphy, 1997, p.156.

14   Biggs, 1997, p.107.

15   Julian Swann, p.20 in William Doyle (Ed), 2001.

16   Geoffrey Treasure, 1985 *The Making of Modern Europe (1648-1780)*, p.303, Methuen & Co Ltd, London.

17   Geoffrey Treasure, op cit, 1985, p.303.

18   Quoted in most works on John Law – for example, Montgomery Hyde, p.217, Williams, p.182.

19   John Law *Money and Trade Considered*, 1705, Internet version, p.23.

20   Antonio Serra, Italian mercantilist, quoted in Stoll, E, *A History Of Economic Thought* (5th ed.), p.52, Faber and Faber, London, 1992.

21   Doyle, 1978.

22   See pages 58 and 66 in Charles Rist's work *History of Monetary And Credit Theory*, George Allen & Unwin, London, 1940.

23   James 2002, p.67.

24   Quoted by Andrews, 1978, p.106.

25   Pevitt, p.256.

26   Clifton, 1995, p.94.

27   Clifton, 1995, p.94.

28   Minton, p.332.

29   Second Inaugural Address of Abraham Lincoln, 4th March 1865.

30   Richard Bonney, *Oxford Dictionary of National Biography*, Vol 32. p.759.

31   Henry Wiencek, *An Imperfect God: George Washington, His Slaves and the Creation of America*, Macmillan, London, 2004.

32   John Law, quoted in Harsin (Ed) Vol 3, pp.98-9.

33   John Law, *Proposals and Reasons,* 1701. pp.276-277.

34   Quoted in Lande/Erlich 1980, p.36.

35   J Shield Nicholson, *A Treatise on Money and Essays on Monetary Problems,* 6th Ed. p.168, London 1918.

The John Law Trail

1   Lauriston Castle: An Edinburgh villa. City of Edinburgh Museums and Galleries, 1999.

2   Montgomery Hyde, p.123.

3   H R Goss, 2000, 'How John Law's Failed Experiment Gave Us a New Word: "Millionaire". Culture Society News, *Wall Street Journal,* 19/7/2000.

4   Wood, p.58.

5   Montgomery Hyde, p.125

6   Wood, p.45.

7   Pevitt, p.264.

8   Daniel Defoe.

9   Duclos, p.266.

10   Duclos pp.265-66.

11   Wood, p.49.

12   Pevitt, p.264.

13   "Roué" Love to Know 1911, *Online Encyclopaedia,* 2004.

14   Daridan, quoted in Minton, 1975, p.270.

15   Halloran, 1997, p.23.

16   Minton p.270.

17   *Portrait of Louisiana*, p.17.

18   Samuel E Morison, Henry S Commager and
     William E Leuchtenburg, *The Growth of the
     American Republic*, (Vol 1 – 7th Ed), p.338, Oxford
     University Press, 1980.

19   John A Garraty, *The American Nation: A History of
     the United States* (9th Ed), p. 167, Longman, New
     York, 1998.

20   Venezia – Church of San Moisé, Visitors notes
     (English version), 2004.

21   Gleeson, 1999, p.200.

22   Quoted by Hyde, p.207.

Bibliography

Andrews, Stuart, *Eighteenth Century Europe: The 1630s to 1815* (6th impression), Longman, 1978.

Baird, Rosemary, *Mistress of the House (1670-1830)*, Phoenix, London, 2003.

Betts, Benjamin, *A Descriptive List Of The Medals Relating To John Law And The Mississippi System: With An Attempt At The Translation Of Their Legends and Inscriptions.* MCMVII. Privately printed.

Biggs, Robin, *Early Modern France (1560-1715),* Oxford University Press, 1977.

Black, Jeremy, 'Foreword' for the Yale Edition of Hatton, Ragnhild, *George I,* Yale English Monarchs, Yale University Press, 2001 Edition.

City of Edinburgh Museums and Galleries, *Lauriston Castle: An Edinburgh Villa*, City of Edinburgh Council 1999.

Clifton, Daniel, (Ed. Director) *Chronicle of America*, Dorling Kindersley Ltd, London, 1995.

Davidson, Marshall, *A Concise History Of France,* Cassell, London, 1971.

Dickens, Charles (Jr), *Dickens's Dictionary of London,* 1879.

Doyle, William, *The Old European Order (1660-1800),* Oxford University Press, Oxford, 1978.

Duclos, Charles P *Secret Memoirs Of The Regency,* Meras (Translator), Greening & Co Ltd, London, 1912.

Gerhold, Dorian, *Westminster Hall: Nine Hundred Years of History,* James and James, London, 1999.

Gleeson, Janet, *The Moneymaker: The true story of a philanderer, gambler, murderer…and the father of modern finance,* Bantam Press, London, 1999.

Glendinning, Victoria, *Jonathan Swift,* Hutchinson, London, 1998.

Haley, K H D, *The Dutch in the Seventeenth Century,* Thames and Hudson, London, 1972.

Halloran, Brian, M, *The Scots College Paris (1603-1792),* John Donald Publishers Ltd, Edinburgh, 1997.

Harsin, P (Ed) *John Law, Oeuvres completes,* Vols 1-111. Printed in Paris 1934. (Reprinted 1980.)

Hervey, Lord John, Some materials towards memoirs of the reign of King George II, in R. Redgwick, 3 vols 1931.

Holmes, Richard, *Redcoat: The British Soldier In The Age of Horse and Musket,* Harper Collins, London, 2001.

Horne, Alistair, *Seven Ages of Paris: Portrait of A City,* London, Macmillan, 2002.

Hutton, Alfred, *The Sword And The Centuries,* Greenhill Books, London, 2002.

Jager, E *The Last Duel: A True Story of Crime, Scandal and Trial by Combat in Medieval France*, Century Books, 2005.

James, Colin, *The Great Nation: France from Louis XV to Napoleon,* The Penguin Press, 2002.

Lande, Lawrence, M. *Banque Royale & Compagnie Des Indes: A Bibliographical Monograph* (With an Introduction by Izzy Ehrlich), Montreal 1980.

Lande, Lawrence, M, *The Rise and Fall of John Law (1716-1720),* McLennan Library, McGill University, Montreal, 1982.

Law, John, 'Money and Trade Considered With the Proposal for Supplying the Nation with Money', Andrew Anderson Printer, Edinburgh, 1705.

Marshall, Alfred, *Money, Credit and Commerce,* London, 1924.

McFarland Davis, M, *A Historical Study of Law's System,* Press of Geo H Ellis, 141 Franklin Street, Boston, 1887. (Reprinted from the *Quarterly Journal of Economics,* April 1887.)

Minton, Robert *John Law: The Father of Paper Money,* Association Press, New York, 1975.

Montgomery Hyde, H, *John Law: a biography,* W H Allen, London, 1969.

Murphy, Antoin, E, *John Law: Economic Theorist and Policy Maker,* Clarendon Press, Oxford, 1997.

O'Gorman, Frank, *The Long Eighteenth Century: British Political and Social History 1688-1832,* Oxford University Press, London, 1997.

Pevitt, Christine, *The Man Who Would Be King: The Life of Philippe d'Orléans, Regent of France*, Phoenix Giant, London, 1997.

Rude, George, *Europe in the Eighteenth Century: Aristocracy and the Bourgeois Challenge*, Weidenfeld & Nicholson, London, 1972.

Sani, Bernardina, 'Rosalba Carriera' in *The Dictionary of Art*, Volume 5, Macmillan Publishers Ltd, London, 1996.

Schama, Simon, *A History of Britain: The British Wars 1603-1776*, BBC Worldwide Ltd, London, 2001.

Southgate, George, *A Textbook Of Modern European History (1643-1848)*, J M Dent & Sons, London, 1949.

St Aubyn, Fiona, *Ackerman's Illustrated London*, Wordsworth Editions Ltd, Ware, 1985.

Stewart, Iain, 'Montesquieu in England: his "Notes on England", with Commentary and Translation, (2002) Oxford University Comparative Law Forum 6, at ouclf.iuscomp.org

Upton, Anthony, F, *Europe 1600-1789*, Arnold, Hodder Headline Group, London, 2001.

Valdez, Stephen, *An Introduction To Global Financial Markets* (3rd Ed.), Macmillan Business, London, 1998.

Williams, Jonathan, (Ed), *Money: A History*, The British Museum Press, 1997.

Wood, J P, *Memoirs of the Life of John Law of Lauriston*, Edinburgh, 1824.

Index